Securing Cloud and Mobility

A Practitioner's Guide

Securing Cloud and Mobility

A Practitioner's Guide

Ian Lim

E. Coleen Coolidge

Paul Hourani

CRC Press
Taylor & Francis Group
Boca Raton   London   New York

CRC Press is an imprint of the
Taylor & Francis Group, an **Informa** business
AN AUERBACH BOOK

CRC Press
Taylor & Francis Group
6000 Broken Sound Parkway NW, Suite 300
Boca Raton, FL 33487-2742

© 2013 by Taylor & Francis Group, LLC
CRC Press is an imprint of Taylor & Francis Group, an Informa business

No claim to original U.S. Government works

Printed in the United States of America on acid-free paper
Version Date: 2012920

International Standard Book Number: 978-1-4398-5055-8 (Hardback)

This book contains information obtained from authentic and highly regarded sources. Reasonable efforts have been made to publish reliable data and information, but the author and publisher cannot assume responsibility for the validity of all materials or the consequences of their use. The authors and publishers have attempted to trace the copyright holders of all material reproduced in this publication and apologize to copyright holders if permission to publish in this form has not been obtained. If any copyright material has not been acknowledged please write and let us know so we may rectify in any future reprint.

Library of Congress Cataloging-in-Publication Data

Lim, Ian.
    Securing cloud and mobility : a practitioner's guide / Ian Lim, Paul Hourani, E. Coleen Coolidge.
        p. cm.
    Includes bibliographical references and index.
    ISBN 978-1-4398-5055-8 (hardback)
    1. Cloud computing--Security measures. 2. Mobile computing--Security measures. I. Hourani, Paul. II. Coolidge, E. Coleen. III. Title.

QA76.585.L56 2012
005.8--dc23

2012036919

Visit the Taylor & Francis Web site at
http://www.taylorandfrancis.com

and the CRC Press Web site at
http://www.crcpress.com

For Baby Kaden, Alexander, and Danielle

Contents

PART II DECONSTRUCTING CLOUD SECURITY

PART III SECURING PRIVATE CLOUD COMPUTING

List of Figures

List of Tables

PART I
RETHINKING IT AND SECURITY

The ancient Greek philosopher Heraclitus declared, "The only constant is change." This is especially true in the world of IT, where change is not only constant, but rapid and disruptive. Cloud computing and mobility fall easily within the category of disruptive technologies that are changing the way we conduct business, organize our workforce, and cater to our customers. This section starts by introducing key concepts around cloud computing—a loaded word used loosely in today's IT-speak. We will deconstruct the terminology of cloud computing to illustrate the breadth and depth of this term. We then discuss the advent of mobility and how it impacts information security. Next, we cover the emerging threat landscape to both cloud and mobility.

We are writing from the point of view of information security practitioners who deal with real-world challenges on a daily basis. We do not have the luxury of unlimited budget to execute ivory tower ideas. We make decisions based on imperfect information. We are constantly prioritizing our resources against risk and business value. Our perspective is told from the trenches. We hope that this section resonates with your own struggles and provides some practical wisdom to better navigate the undulating terrains of cloud and mobility.

1

TECTONIC SHIFTS

1.1 Disruptive Forces

We have all been bombarded by cloud computing and mobility in the past year. We have heard it from our executive who walked through the door with the newest gadget and wants it on the company's network *pronto*. We've been asked by our marketing division to provision the entire department with Mac® computers. We find out, after the fact, that our development team has procured capabilities on Amazon® Web Services (AWS) and is putting company information assets in the public cloud. Every major security conference we attend has helpful servings of cloud and mobility sessions.

These disruptive technologies are not buzzwords that are on the hype cycle 1 minute, but are replaced by other trends the next. They matter because they fundamentally alter how people interact with technology. The evolution at the consumer level will inadvertently lead companies to transform their IT to meet customer expectations. Needless to say, major changes in the IT landscape will have significant impact on information security. Security practitioners will have to evolve their old paradigms to contend with the forces of cloud computing and mobility.

1.2 Deconstructing Cloud Computing

1.2.1 NIST Definition

There is a plethora of definitions for cloud computing, from slick marketing buzzwords to highly technical terms. The most authoritative definition comes from the National Institute of Standards and Technology in its Special Publication 800-145 (NIST SP 800-145):

> Cloud computing is a model for enabling ubiquitous, convenient, on-demand network access to a shared pool of configurable computing

resources (e.g., networks, servers, storage, applications, and services) that can be rapidly provisioned and released with minimal management effort or service provider interaction.

Let's break this down (see Table 1.1).

1.2.2 The Three Service Models

In addition to the NIST definition, you need to understand the three different cloud service models and four cloud deployment models to get the full flavor of the term *cloud computing*.

The three service models to cloud computing are:

- Software as a service (SaaS): An on-demand service that is hosted in the cloud. This service is specific to a vertical, such as human resources, sales, etc. Upkeep is minimal for SaaS, as everything is taken care of by the service provider. Key examples include Salesforce, Service Now, and Workday.
- Platform as a service (PaaS): This model is largely targeted at the development community. It provides it with a solution stack for a specific code platform to develop, test, and deploy its web applications. No infrastructure knowledge is required to use PaaS, and some providers enable hosting to push code into production on the web. Examples include Google's App Engine, Microsoft's Azure, and Heroku.
- Infrastructure as a service (IaaS): Instead of a specific service or platform, IaaS provides ease of provisioning and de-provisioning virtual servers. Basically, it's like the old data center hosting services without having to deal with physical servers. Instead of renting a cage for your servers, you use a portal to select how many virtual machines you want and where. You have to plan your virtual infrastructure and separate your environments. The uptake on this model by the enterprise has largely been relegated to testing and disaster recovery sites. Small- to medium-sized businesses run their production environment in this model. Examples include Amazon Web Services (which also provides some PaaS capabilities), Teremark Enterprise Cloud (now Verizon), and GoGrid.

Table 1.1 NIST Definition of Cloud

NIST DEFINITION	NOTES
Cloud computing is a model...	Cloud computing has three service models and four deployment models. The three service models are infrastructure as a service (IaaS), platform as a service (PaaS), and software as a service (SaaS). The four deployment models are public cloud, private cloud, community cloud, and hybrid cloud.
to enable...	The holy grail of cloud computing is to do IT cheaper, faster, and better. Cheaper because you can leverage economies of scale and only pay for what you use as opposed to sizing your data center to peak usage. Faster because you do not have to build your own infrastructure, platforms, or services. Better is a relative term, but essentially cloud platforms have agility, performance, capacity, and feature sets that rival most in-house IT infrastructures. That said, there are significant limitations to cloud as well—information security being a chief concern.
ubiquitous...	As opposed to being limited by your IT perimeters, wide area network connections, and point-to-point leased lines. Cloud means that you are reachable from the Internet by everyone, everywhere. This could be a detriment as well. With the rise of hacktivism and well-funded highly sophisticated cyber criminals, being ubiquitous also means putting a big target on your back.
convenient...	Most major cloud companies have the ability to provide computing resources through a management interface that you can easily access. The prepackaged options can be ordered and provisioned instantly.
on-demand...	This is a contrast to the old provisioning model where physical servers have to be ordered, racked, and configured to be functional. On-demand means that resources are available instantaneously.
network access to a shared pool...	In cloud, different groups have access to common resources. In IT terms, we call this multitenancy. Tenants could be different customers in a public or community cloud, or different business divisions in a private cloud. There are significant security concerns and guidelines around multitenancy that we will address later.
of configurable computing resources...	This implies the various layers of virtualization—server, network, application, storage, and services.
that can be rapidly provisioned...	Advancement in virtualization has brought orchestration to the vocabulary of IT professionals. Secure orchestration is the ability to auto-provision network, system, and application layers for multiple tenants while keeping the security context intact. Without orchestration, there will be no on-demand. The key limitation of cloud orchestration is the lack of customization.
and released with minimal management effort or service provider interaction.	This is done via management or customer interfaces that leverage orchestration technologies to rapidly provision virtual servers, platforms, and services in a predefined manner.

1.2.3 The Four Deployment Models

The four cloud computing deployment models are:

- Public cloud: All infrastructure and services are owned and maintained by the provider. You pay a set fee to use the provider's services. This is typically the most cost-effective model due to economy of scale, but it is likely the least secure model due to the one-size-fits-all approach and the security implications of multitenancy.
- Private cloud: You own and maintain the entire infrastructure. Internal virtual server farms can be considered a private cloud if the on-demand and elasticity feature is available to various business units in a multitenant fashion. This is typically the most expensive model. The security of this deployment is dependent on the company's Infosec team and its budget.
- Community cloud: This is a variation of the public cloud model except it is more targeted toward a specific industry vertical. While the public cloud deployment model is highly accessible, the community cloud might only limit access to its customers via virtual private network (VPN) or hard-line connections. The community cloud also builds its infrastructure and services to meet the needs of the community it is targeting. For example, in the financial services community cloud, there will be a high emphasis on governance, risk, and compliance, as opposed to a public cloud model where you have barebones security. Community cloud deployments are on the rise because it provides a good balance between economy of scale and controls that meet the specific industry's requirements.
- Hybrid cloud: This deployment must include at least one instance of private cloud and an instance of public cloud that are connected in some fashion. This approach is used to leverage specific functions of the public cloud while maintaining control over defined data and compute capabilities within the private cloud. For example, some companies might run their entire business operations within their private cloud, but send their archive functions into the public cloud. Other companies might use the public cloud as an extension of their private cloud to provide bursting capabilities during peak seasons.

1.3 The Rise of Mobility

In the past couple of years, iOS and Android devices in the form of smart phones and tablets have made a seismic imprint on our consumer and business world. While these devices have not replaced laptops, they have grown in such numbers that IT organizations cannot stem the wave of requests for adoption of this novel technology or stop unauthorized devices from connecting to the corporate network. Many of you may stand your ground and are able to stem the tide of mobility, but when a senior executive walks in with his or her iPad, or when the marketing department makes a strong business case for tablets, the battle line starts to erode and eventually you're overtaken with managing multiple flavors of iOS and Android across the enterprise.

We would advocate not standing in front of the mobility train. It will no doubt run us over and drag our ragged bodies for miles, and here's why: mobility has successfully won over the consumer market. Apple's 2011 Annual Report[1] reported 72 million units were sold in 2011, compared to 39 million in 2010.[2] Apple sold 32 million iPads in 2011 compared to 7 million in 2010. That's a whopping 334% growth in the span of a year, and that number is rising into 2012 (Figure 1.1). These numbers make iOS devices a formidable transformative force at the enterprise level. Companies are rallying to the iOS platform to reach their consumers. With that comes application development in iOS, which, by the way, brings Mac OSX into the enterprise.

Android devices are not far behind either; however, because the OS is supported by a plethora of hardware devices, getting a detailed count is difficult. Asymco, a market research company specializing in mobility, projected the number of Android devices in the market based on Google's reported activation count of the Android OS. The

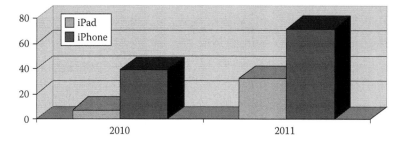

Figure 1.1 iPhone® and iPad® growth in millions.

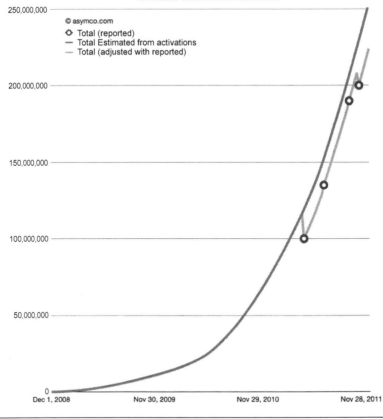

Figure 1.2   Android growth as reported by http://www.asymco.com.

chart in Figure 1.2 reflects tremendous growth in the Android space, rivaling that of iOS devices. Based on projections, around 224 to 253 million Android devices in the market are estimated as of 2011.[3]

What is the significance of all these statistics? It means that our workforce and our customers are embracing iOS and Android in record numbers. These mobile innovations are changing the way we work and live. Consequentially, the mobility agenda will strain our existing IT infrastructure and force its transformation to support the new norm. Most of us have already experienced the scenario where a senior marketing executive walks in with his or her iPad and demands that you connect it to the network. After that comes your development manager asking for a group of developers to have iOS and Android platforms to build mobile applications. This is followed by myriad subdivisions within your company that want to be enabled with tablets for business purposes.

We have to get ahead of the curve, as opposed to being a bystander reacting to this revolution. Some of you may attempt to step in front of this speeding train and enforce restrictive policies around mobility to curb its expansion in your enterprise. Not a good idea. While there are significant issues with mobility, it is not and must not be the enemy of security. The new economy requires that we enable our workforce to be more successful with these devices by securing them, not stopping them.

To be effective, we need to understand the attack surfaces created by our mobile enterprise users and establish a methodology to effectively reduce the risk in this space. We have to understand the implications of bring your own device (BYOD) and where we stand in this debate. We need to build repeatable workflows to equip whole departments with mobile capabilities while protecting our data assets. We need to understand how to establish a secure mobile application development platform. We need to know how to build secure IT infrastructure to host consumer-facing mobile applications or revisit our existing infrastructure to retrofit it for mobility. We will provide a practitioner's guide to these topics in later chapters.

1.4 New IT

Cloud and mobility have not only changed the landscape of IT, but also reshaped consumer and enterprise expectations. Today, consumers expect ubiquitous computing, which translates to having access to their applications/data anytime, anywhere, and on any device. Companies that want to expand their market share will push their IT to deliver according to these new consumer expectations. The days of limiting the flow of data or locking the enterprise to company-issued devices are waning and left to the high-security organizations. Due to the tectonic shifts in the realms of cloud and mobility, security practitioners have to evolve from a lockdown mindset and embrace a paradigm that enables the business to have agility and ubiquity while maintaining a sound security posture.

References

1. Apple. 2011 10K annual report, filed October 26, 2011. http://investor. apple.com/secfiling.cfm?filingID=1193125-11-282113&CIK=320193.
2. Apple. 2010 10K annual report, filed October 27, 2011. http://investor. apple. com/secfiling.cfm?filingID=1193125-10-238044&CIK=320193.
3. Horace Dediu. How many Android phones have been activated? Accessed June 27, 2012, http://www.asymco.com/2011/12/21/how -many-android-phones-have-been-activated/.

2

THE EVOLVING THREAT LANDSCAPE

We covered the disruptive technologies in IT, but the world of information security is rapidly changing as well. The discovery of the Stuxnet virus pushed cyber espionage into the vocabulary of the information security community. The proliferation of hacktivisim (where hacking meets activism) and the prominence of Anonymous in the news have brought fresh fears of distributed denial of service (DDoS) attacks and highly targeted attacks into the forefront of top security concerns. Ever present are growing threats from organized crime and new attack surfaces exposed by cloud and mobility. In this chapter, we will make a case that information security has evolved significantly, and we as security practitioners have to adjust our old world thinking to fit a new breed of attack vectors.

2.1 From Cryptographers to World Leaders

In 1991, a group of about 50 cryptographers gathered in a ballroom at Hotel Sofitel in Redwood City to share knowledge and trade stories in a little known event called Cryptography, Standards and Public Policy. This was the inception of what is now the largest security gathering in the world—the RSA Conference. Back then, the term *information security* was only used in academic circles and the military. Security incidents were caused by geeks flexing their hacking muscles. In most companies, the information security functions were buried deep within networking departments or spread across system administrators. There were very few regulations or industry standards around protecting digital data. Information security occupied zero mind space in the public arena and had little to no playtime in the press.

Fast-forward 20 years. The RSA Conference is now held in three continents: the Americas, Europe, and Asia. The final keynote speaker for RSA San Francisco 2011 was President Bill Clinton. For 2012, it has secured speakers such as Robert S. Mueller, head of the FBI, and ex-British Prime Minister Tony Blair. Information security topics are being discussed on CNN, in *The New York Times*, and every other major media powerhouse. Espionage, hacktivism, and data breaches are making prime time news at least once a month. The top three best-selling novels on *USA Today* for 2011 have a hacker as the main character (*The Girl with the Dragon Tattoo*, *The Girl Who Played with Fire*, and *The Girl Who Kicked the Hornet's Nest*). To add fuel to fire, a significant number of laws, regulations, and industry standards have come into effect within the last 10 years to put information security front and center in various enterprises, governments, and within the consumer space. These laws and industry standards are still being deliberated and more are being passed each quarter.

When Bill Clinton spoke at RSA in 2011, it marked that information security had come into the mainstream. We have not only gained legitimacy in the eyes of information technology, but we have risen above IT into the realm of social dialogue. Information security is no longer an obscure technical topic that is being discussed in ivory towers or behind closed doors by cryptographers. It has weaved its way into the daily lives of ordinary people, impacted companies in significant ways, and mobilized nation-states to address the growing concern of cyber threats.

2.2 The Changing Threat Landscape

When we develop our security strategy for a new year, we draw from four major areas: pain points, business strategy, changes in compliance requirements, and the current threat landscape. Pain point is where you look at the past year to highlight key areas of improvements. Reviewing business strategy is aligning your strategy to support management objectives. Taking into account the changes in compliance requirements is about surveying the horizon for new regulations and industry standards that may impact your information security program. Last but not least, the threat landscape considers the prevalent and up-and-coming trends in cyber threats.

The threat landscape is constantly changing. In the 1990s, we had hackers that were flexing their cyber muscles to outdo each other in a game of digital bravado. The late 1990s into the early 2000s were dominated by the presence of worms, and companies were plagued with mass virus outbreaks. The late 2000s saw the rise of organized crime exploiting the burgeoning e-commerce economy to steal and monetize nonpublic personal information. In our current decade we are seeing the age of hacktivism, where targeted organizations are being harassed with DDoS and data breaches to prove a point. Cyber terrorism and state-sponsored cyber espionage in the form of breaches to military databases, as well as viruses, target critical infrastructure such as nuclear power plants, in the case of Stuxnet. Table 2.1 demonstrates the evolution of threat through the recent decades.

Every threat begins with the attacker. Each attacker has specific motives and targets. His or her *modus operandi* also varies due to his or her objectives. In Figure 2.1 is a simple graphical representation that encapsulates the attacker profiles. Let's take a look at each group individually to examine its motives, targets, and *modus operandi*.

Table 2.1 Internet Threat Evolution

1990s	2000s	TODAY
Weeks between vulnerability announcement and exploits in the wild	Days between vulnerability announcement and exploits in the wild	Hours between vulnerability announcement and exploits in the wild
Self-propagating worms	Blended threats	Advance persistent threats
Script kiddies hack to impress their peers	Organized criminals hack for financial gains	Hacktivists hack to make a point; cyber espionage is a reality
Denial of service (DoS) disrupting websites	Botnets used for extortion and spamming	Voluntary botnets; email data posted on public websites
Sniff wireless traffic and capitalize on unprotected wireless access points	Exploit wireless infrastructure to compromise internal networks	App-based attacks on Apple and Android devices
Insider threat comes from employees that work in your facilities	Insider threat comes from business partners, contractors, outsourcers, and consultants	Insider threat comes from cloud service providers

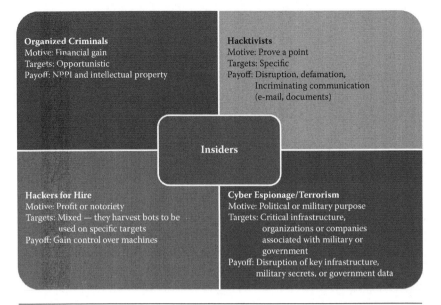

Figure 2.1 Profiles of attackers.

2.3 Hacktivists

2.3.1 *Motivation*

Hacktivism is a term used to describe the movement of a breed of hackers who hack out of conviction, thus hacker + activist. Hacktivism has been on a steady rise in the past few years, stealing the limelight from data breaches. The term *hacker* is loosely used, as it may conjure up the idea that every person that subscribes to hacktivism is security savvy and highly skilled. The reality is closer to clusters of elite hackers loosely coupled under a brand that mobilizes the masses by rallying them toward a common goal and providing them the appropriate time, place, and tools to launch a specific mass attack.

Their motives are anchored on causes. In the wake of the Arab Spring movement, hacktivism took the form of using social media to organize demonstrations, as well as communicate to the world at large the plight of the activists. Some targeted attacks were launched against government sites in protest. In the case of hacking groups Anonymous and LulzSec, activities within these groups are driven by what is termed *lulz*. Lulz is a derivative of LOL, which stands for "laughing out loud." The essence of the phrase "Doing it for the lulz" is to convey the idea of hacking as a kind of farce to highlight an injustice or a contradiction without taking it too seriously. A good example of this was the hacktivism that took place against the Church of Scientology for its attempt to censor the Internet. DDoS attacks were carried out against the Church of Scientology websites. Prank calls and live protests were held in front of churches and were broadcast over social media. A site was established called Project Chanology (named after the notorious 4chan website, which allows for uncensored dialogue) to provide resources, ideas, and a platform for acts against scientology. This level of protest generated a significant following and press coverage. The Church of Scientology probably spent a significant amount of money thwarting these attacks and taking legal action.

2.3.2 Modus Operandi

Essentially, hacktivists rally around causes and their targets are usually companies or organizations or specific individuals who push an agenda contrary to the pathos of the hacktivists. If your company evokes the wrath of hacktivists, you need to brace yourself for the significant onslaught of unpredictable attacks. Here are two prevalent methods used by major hacktivist groups:

- E-mail or communication data: Hacktivists are looking to expose their target and paint it in a bad light. E-mail communication that is stolen and published widely on the Internet is an effective method to humiliate the target. This was seen in the case of HB Gary's ex-CEO Aaron Barr, who made the mistake of claiming that he could unveil Anonymous's ring leaders. His company e-mail was hacked and published on the Internet, along with web defacement and a DDoS attack on his business. The net effect of the attack was that he had to step down from his executive position and go into hiding. Another very powerful instance of a data-driven attack was seen in the infamous leak of 251,287 State Department confidential cables to Wikileaks.
- DDoS attacks: Hacktivists distribute tools (like Low Orbital Ion Cannon (LOIC)) and provide tutorials on how to converge on their targets. Hacktivists have the ability to form

voluntary botnets that can be used to interrupt key government sites such as the Department of Justice and the Federal Bureau of Investigation, as was done in the wake of the shutdown of Megaupload.

• Publicity attacks: Hacktivists are masters of media manipulation. Their potency lies in their power to rally a herd behind their causes or publicize their activities to the masses through social media. They have even broken the barriers to getting their message out through mainstream news channels.

2.3.3 Hacktivism and Cloud

There are three current implications to hacktivism and the cloud: cloud as a target, cloud as a service, and cloud as a platform.

First, the cloud is a high-value target for hacktivists. Cloud providers have a number of tenants, which gives hacktivists a big bang for their buck. Cloud providers also can be accessed publicly, as well as from within. Hacktivists can sign up for cloud services and attack the system from within. Cloud providers are also notorious for not having sound security. Their focus is to leverage the economy of scale to provide capabilities in the most cost-efficient ways. Security is often a necessary evil or an afterthought. Hacktivists can exploit the lack of security in a cloud provider to further their goals.

Second, the cloud provides services that are useful to hackers. One great example is demonstrated by the notorious hacktivist group called LulzSec, which signed on for services on Cloudflare, a content distribution network. In June 2, 2011,[1] LulzSec used a free subscription offered by Cloudflare to host its website: www.lulzsecurity.com. As noted earlier, Cloudflare offers DDoS protection and anonymity to its subscribers. LulzSec proceeded to publicize its Sony hack on its lulzsecurity website from behind Cloudflare. It posted information about a million user accounts stolen from the Sony website to the public Internet. This brought on a response from other hacker communities to conduct a DDoS attack on the lulzsecurity website, which brought it down, but it was restored in 45 minutes due to the use of Cloudflare. The long and short of this story is that cloud services along with social networking tools are used heavily by hacktivists.

They are extremely Internet savvy and know power of the cloud better than most of us.

Last, the cloud is used as a platform by hacktivists to distribute code, announce their exploits, meet and exchange ideas, etc. Hacktivists gather and mobilize within the cloud. This often puts cloud providers in a quandary, as in the case of Cloudflare. Do they prohibit any type of hacking activities within their cloud services? Do they violate their users' privacy in order to spy on hacktivists? The cloud is the platform in which most "hacktivistic" activities are launched.

2.3.4 Hacktivism and Mobility

Outside of using mobile apps such as Twitter to mobilize, inform, and publicize their exploits, hacktivists have not actively tapped into mobility as a vector or vehicle of attack. This is by no means an indication of what might happen in the future. Potential scenarios could be developing and publishing rogue mobile applications that steal personal data and photos to post and humiliate their targets on the public web, or even to use as leverage for negotiations. Other avenues could be to infiltrate the target organization's e-mail infrastructure using mobile access to e-mail and calendaring. Another avenue is to penetrate an organization's internal network via the application programming interfaces (APIs) of mobile applications. Part V, "Securing Mobile," is dedicated to discussing the vulnerabilities and defense strategies against threats for mobile computing.

2.3.5 Hacktivism and Security

Rethinking security in the age of hacktivism requires us to consider the following defense measures:

- Protect private communication data: As security practitioners, we are vigilant about nonpublic personal information (NPPI), credit card, and intellectual property data. We need to start considering attacks on private communication data, e.g., e-mails, voicemails, text messages, cables, confidential memos, etc. These are going to be targeted to incriminate and possibly shame your organization. Another method is to push awareness to steer how company private communication is created.

- Establish defense against distributed denial of service (DDoS): There are four general methods to counter a DDoS attack. One of the most effective is to use a content distribution network (CDN) to protect your websites. Essentially, you change your domain name resolution to the CDN provider who has the bandwidth to absorb and counter DDoS attacks. Another similar way is to buy DDoS protection from your Internet service provider. The third way is to do it yourself and get in-line DDoS protection appliances to filter legitimate traffic from DDoS traffic. Lastly (and most ineffective), you can buy firewall products that claim to offer DDoS protection.

- Revamp your security incident response process: If your organization could be a potential target for hacktivists, you need to work through your damage control scenario with your executives, legal, and public relations teams. The blitz of a hacktivistic publicity attack could be curbed or slowed by an effective counterblitz by your own public relations and sales departments. You need to reach the media and your customers with key messages to minimize reputational damage.

- Conduct due care before putting your data in the cloud: Hackers are both using and targeting cloud service providers. Being on the same hardware may expose you to internal-based attacks. Being in the cloud makes you an easy or collateral target to attacks on that cloud provider or its key clients. You need to perform due care on your business units before they take company capabilities or data into a public cloud. Part IV of this book provides examples of workflows to conduct internal due diligence prior to allowing cloud services in your organization.

2.4 Organized Cyber Crime

2.4.1 Motivation

While hacktivism is making headlines, cyber crime conducted by organized crime is still the most prevalent threat to our information security posture. The motive of cyber criminals can be summed up in one word: money. Once the criminals figured out how to monetize information assets stolen from the digital economy, the cyber criminals became more organized and launched more sophisticated operations. The Identity Theft Resource Center reported 419 data breaches and 22,918,441 records stolen for 2011.[2] Symantec reported that cyber criminals stole $114 billion[3] in 2010, and the cost of recovery from these exploits tallied up to $274 billion for companies and individuals. In another study, the Ponemon Institute conducted a survey of 50 organizations, and the median annualized cost attributed to cyber crime is $5.9 million per year[4] for each company. These numbers should convey how committed and serious these organized cyber criminals are in getting to your systems and data assets.

2.4.2 Modus Operandi

The 2011 "Data Breach Investigations Report" (DBIR) conducted by Verizon, the U.S. Secret Service, and the Dutch High Tech Crime Unit identifies the sources of these breaches (Figure 2.2).

The statistics show that a majority of the cyber attacks' IP addresses originate from Eastern Europe, in particular Russia and Turkey. These figures may indicate that the Eastern Europe region has both the human capital and infrastructure to launch sophisticated cyber attacks as an ongoing "business" operation. In a report entitled "Cybercrime Attribution: An Eastern European Case Study," written by Stephen McCombie,[5] the researcher points out that Russia's major crime families have deep investments in cyber crime. We are not dealing with hacktivists causing mayhem from their home PCs. According to McCombie, these organized criminals operate data centers for phishing, spamming, botnet command and control networks, and a plethora of cyber criminal activities. Another article by Jarrod Rifkind[6] indicates that Russian organized crime families were recruited from ex-employees of the Russian Federal Agency for

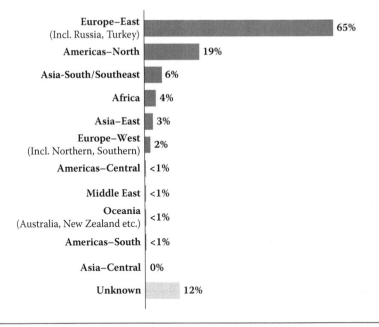

Figure 2.2 Origins of data breaches.

Government Communications and Information (FAPSI) when the agency disbanded in 2003. The Eastern European cyber criminals not only have enterprise-grade infrastructure, but highly qualified computer experts with deep technical experience, insider knowledge, and key contacts within the government. We are up against a formidable enemy with our shrinking IT security budget.

2.4.3 Organized Crime and Cloud

The Cisco 2011 Annual Security Report[7] indicates that cyber criminals are looking at cloud and mobility to be promising profit centers in the near future (Figure 2.3).

Organized criminals are profit driven and opportunistic. Cloud is appealing for the following reasons:

- Big payoff and multitenancy: The cloud provides a big target for cyber criminals willing to invest resources and infrastructure to gain a profit. Sony Playstation's breach of 77 million customer records is an example of hacking a cloud service that yields a significant payoff. While this incident

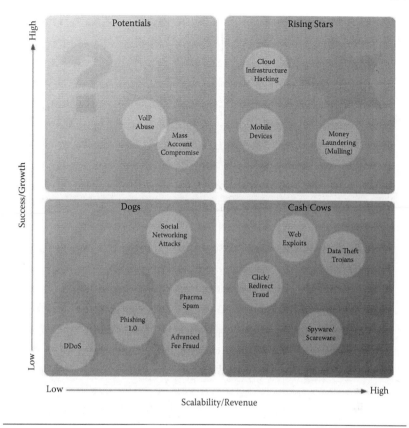

Figure 2.3 Cisco® cyber crime return on investment matrix.

was not attributed to organized crime, it points to the fact that cloud services are treasure troves of data. Additionally, the multitenant environment of the cloud increases the return on investment (ROI) for the effort required to break in to a cloud provider.

- Cost of security: Cloud providers leverage the economy of scale to make a bigger margin. Security is an added cost and takes away from their bottom line. Major cloud service providers such as Paypal and Apple's iCloud may make the necessary investments and expertise in information security to protect NPPI data, but this might not be the case for a number of lesser known cloud companies that are jumping on the cloud profit bandwagon. Take, for example, credit card processing companies that are either offering cloud services or hosting their production systems on a public cloud or both. The extent of their security may be to pass the Payment Card Industry Data Security Standard (PCI-DSS), which is reasonable security, but any seasoned security practitioner knows that an audit is only as good as the qualified security assessor (QSA) doing it. Having a pass on your report of compliance (ROC) greatly helps, but it does not guarantee protection from a well-funded, sophisticated organized cyber criminal group targeting your information assets. Verizon's "Data Breach Investigations Report" shows that 11% of its data breach caseload was PCI-DSS compliant at the time of the breach.[8]

- Immaturity of cloud security: Cloud security hinges on the maturity of securing virtualized infrastructures. Some of these technologies are still being developed or are in beta. Vendors are starting to bring encryption of virtual instances, along with its data elements, to cloud service providers, but this is not a widely adopted or available capability to customers. Security technologies and practices to effectively segment tenants in a cloud environment are also in their adolescence. In addition to the technology, cloud security is relatively new, and the maturation of frameworks and processes is still being discussed and researched among university and industry forums. There is also a general lack of governance in the cloud security space outside of PCI-DSS and a spate of privacy laws. Cloud providers are not held to additional standards to protect their customers' data assets. Most providers are black boxes that do not allow audits or regular security testing by their customers. All these factors lead to opportunities by highly motivated cyber criminals who understand cloud architecture and have the means to exploit its lack of security.

2.4.4 Organized Crime and Mobility

Organized crime is already active in the mobile device space. Eric Chien from Symantec published a recent 2011 report entitled "Motivations of Recent Android Malware,"[9] which details seven specific schemes targeting the Android mobile devices:

- Premium rate number billing: The cyber criminal registers premium rate numbers and plants a malware within the phone to send SMS messages without the user's knowledge to these premium rate numbers, thus billing the victims.
- Spyware: These rogue mobile applications siphon off pertinent data from the phone, such as contact information, GPS location, e-mails, SMS locations, photos, call logs, etc., and send them off to the cyber criminals. They could come in the form of a functioning game or app with a service running in the background.
- Search engine poisoning: This is a scheme where the attacker uses an Android-based malware to direct artificial search results to a specific mobile website that is owned by the attacker. This in turn increases traffic and hit rates to the attacker's site, thus promoting a favorable rank from search engines. The site's artificial popularity draws ad clicks and revenue for the attacker.
- Pay per click: Similar to nonmobile instantiation of this scheme, the mobile version installs a malware that generates ad clicks on the attacker sites, thus generating revenue. However, the mobile version also has the ability to leverage the carrier's value-added services (such as mobile TV) to generate phone billing in addition to ad clicks.
- Pay per install: This malware has the ability to download other mobile applications, thus generating revenue for certain mobile application distribution marketplaces that may be affiliated with cyber criminals.
- Adware: This malware generates income by displaying ads. Cyber criminals clone popular games and apps to generate ad revenues.
- mTAN stealing: mTAN stands for mobile transaction authentication number. This is the out-of-band authenticator for certain banks to prevent man-in-the-middle attacks. There is malware in the wild that targets the mTAN number specifically.

On the iOS front, there have been a series of vulnerabilities that have been reported in jail-broken phones (a term used to describe running a nonstandard iOS platform by running custom kernels). Fraudsters are distributing iOS malware in jail-broken marketplaces such as Cydia to steal user phone data, including passwords, e-mails, contact information, GPS locations, etc. Germany's Federal Office for Information Security uncovered specific vulnerabilities in the handling of PDF documents and in how iOS does address space layout randomization.[10]

For non-jail-broken iOS devices, Charlie Miller from Accuvant found a bug in iOS that allowed him to craft an app called Instastock to ship address book information back to him.[11] The kicker is that Miller's app was distributed by Apple's App Store, which is supposed to scan all apps for malicious code. Miller was trying to make the point that if he could pass Apple's security to distribute his app to the masses, so can cyber criminals.

Lastly, there's a growing movement in certain countries to use mobile money or mPayments. In mid-2011, Ericsson launched mobile money services allowing mobile phone users to send and receive money from family and friends in seven countries across Europe.[12] Cyber criminals will definitely flock to exploit these capabilities in the near term with a combination of scams and hacks.

2.4.5 Organized Crime and Security

Cyber crime is highly lucrative, has a low cost of entry compared to other crimes, is target rich (global reach), and has a relatively low likelihood of getting caught. These are perfect conditions for organized crime to thrive. That said, law enforcement all over the world have been ramping up their efforts to apprehend these criminals. The FBI worked for 2 years to take down six Estonian nationals who infected 4 million machines in 100 countries with a malware that changed their Domain Name System (DNS) to drive ad clicks.[13] In a different operation, the Department of Justice and the FBI set precedence for "the most complete and comprehensive enforcement action ever taken by U.S authorities to disable an international botnet."[14] Synergies, case laws, and methodologies are being developed to deal with the bane of cyber crime.

We as practitioners need to contribute to this wind of change by

- Increasing our security posture: Cyber crime is about profit. It is our job to prevent our enterprises from being profit centers for these criminals. Raise awareness, build solid layered defense, encrypt or tokenize NPPI, and find and remediate vulnerabilities so that these criminals have to increase their cost to get to your information assets. Make it cost-prohibitive for them to be in this business.

- Cultivating threat intelligence: Participate in roundtables and forum discussions with your peers on a regular basis, especially those in the same industry. Know what is going on in your space. Where possible, consider sharing sanitized threat intelligence data with your security vendors and seek out services that provide big data analytics for threat trends on the Internet at large. Subscribe to RSS feeds, newsletters, vendor threat portals, security pundit blogs, or any informative sources that provide real-time threat data in your space. Gather and correlate threat data from your network intelligently and make threat data actionable via a sound deployment of your security incident event management infrastructure.

- Implementing an effective security incident response process: In light of the sophistication of organized crime attacks, the response process must not only be internally focused, but include participation from global or regional Computer Security Incident Response Teams (CSIRTs) such as FIRST or APCERT. These international CSIRTs bring together government, enterprise, and academic members to provide a collaborative effort against cyber crime.

- Pay attention to mobility: While most of the mobility attacks are targeted at consumers, it is paramount to be ahead of the curve in deploying sound mobile capabilities to your end users as well as building out mobile-facing apps for your consumers.

2.5 Cyber Espionage and Terrorism

2.5.1 Motivation

Cyber warfare is usually reserved for the Department of Defense or targeted at key national infrastructures such as the electric grid, governmental sites, media outlets, or major financial systems. Those of you who are in market segments that may be potential targets to terrorists and state-sponsored hackers should be fully cognizant of their motives and methods.

Cyber espionage takes the state-funded intelligence harvesting and subterfuge activities into connected networks and closed systems. Major countries in the world have recently ramped up their cyber war capabilities. China has "'embraced the idea that successful war-fighting is based on the ability to exert control over an adversary's information and information systems,"[15] states a report published by Northrop Grumman to Congress dated March 7, 2012. This ideology translates to significant investment in recruiting and training technical resources, developing cutting-edge technology, and establishing world-class infrastructure to achieve the goals of cyber warfare. It was no accident that China overtook the United States in building the world's fastest computer on the planet, called Tianhe-1A,[16] in 2010. The Northrop Grumman report confirms that China's capabilities in cyber war "have advanced sufficiently to pose genuine risk to U.S. military operations in the event of a conflict." They could also turn their highly sophisticated cyber weapons on the corporate sector, and our security measures would be no match for their sophistication.

In addition to China, countries like Iran are ramping up their cyber offense capabilities. The BBC recently reported cyber attacks against its broadcasting capabilities.[17] The attacks were largely targeted at their BBC Persian TV broadcasting into Iran, but also included DDoS attacks against e-mail and Internet services. These are instances where the possibility of nation-states attacking corporations is evident and growing.

There is also a growing cyber conflict brewing between Bangladesh and India, where national stock exchanges, banking service, and government sites are being targeted in a steady escalation of conflict between the two countries.[18]

2.5.2 Modus Operandi

In a unique display of ingenuity, the Stuxnet virus emerged in the wild with the specific purpose of infecting very specific supervisory control and data acquisition (SCADA) systems within Iran's nuclear enrichment facilities. This type of targeted attack shows a level of unparalleled sophistication that required a detailed understanding of the target systems being attacked. Security experts speculate that Stuxnet had the support of nation-states. Stuxnet demonstrates that the realms of military and public domain have melded in our interconnected world. We may discover the next Stuxnet-like virus on our corporate network or endpoint devices and potentially be implicated in a clandestine operation to attack critical infrastructures in our country or abroad. In today's changing threat landscape, we as practitioners have to now contend with very smart people who have specific agendas and the expertise and resources to infiltrate our environment to achieve their military objectives. Their M.O. varies from targeted hacking, to worms, to DDoS, to social engineering. Their attacks are well funded, sophisticated, and highly targeted.

2.5.3 Cyber Espionage, Terrorism, and Cloud

Cloud is in the business of centralizing computing resources and services to gain economy of scale and to provide ubiquitous computing. From the perspective of nation-states or terrorists scouring for meaningful information assets or aiming to cause the most significant disruptive activities, cloud service providers become desirable targets. Hacktivists may not have the resources to hack a major cloud provider. Organized crime has the money, but they want a strong ROI for their time and resources. They may weigh the costs and benefits and attack weaker targets if the cloud provider has invested a significant budget in security. Cyber espionage or terrorists have the patience, expertise, and funding to infiltrate key cloud infrastructures and lie dormant until the time is right to strike.

2.5.4 Cyber Espionage, Terrorism, and Mobility

Mobility is typically a means to an end in the arena of cyber espionage and terrorism. A nation-state might want to infect a mobile device for the purposes of pilfering information assets or locating GPS coordinates from specific targets. Similar to Stuxnet, state-sponsored malware may spread in the wild until they get to their desired target prior to activating. This has little bearing on your end users. Terrorists may attack the availability of mobile carriers to disrupt telecommunication capabilities.

2.5.5 Cyber Espionage, Terrorism, and Security

Protection against cyber espionage and terrorism is no different than against hacktivism and cyber criminals. Layered defense and intelligence detection are paramount. With that said, the funding and expertise that is inherent in state-funded attacks might overwhelm our security posture, backed by an ever-shrinking corporate budget.

The Homeland Security Cyber and Physical Infrastructure Protection Act of 2011 is an amendment to the Homeland Security Act of 2002, which facilitated the creation of the Office of Cyber Security and Communications (CS&C).[19] The charter of the CS&C is to enhance the "security, resiliency, and reliability of the nation's cyber and communications infrastructure" by actively engaging the public, private, and international partners to avert and respond to catastrophic cyber incidents. The CS&C partners with the U.S. Computer Emergency Readiness Team (US-CERT) to investigate security incidents that may have national implications. It is imperative that you expand your computer security incident handling process to include the notification of law enforcement and government agencies by engaging US-CERT. In the event of a security incident in your environment that may be deemed as a threat to national security or have the markings of an attack from a terrorist group or a nation-state, go to https://forms.us-cert.gov/report/to submit your incident through the US-CERT Incident Reporting System. If the incident is urgent, contact the following numbers:

- Department of Homeland Security
  - Operator number: 202-282-8000
  - Comment line: 202-282-8495
- US-CERT Security Operations Center
  - Phone: +1 888-282-0870
  - E-mail: soc@us-cert.gov

To be vigilant, check the CS&C's website at http://www.dhs.gov/files/events/cybersecurity.shtm for events and outreach. There are conferences, workshops, and resources offered by the government to spread security awareness. There may also be opportunities to partner with the government and other organizations to build solidarity in our defense against cyber threats.

2.6 Hackers for Hire

2.6.1 Motivation and Modus Operandi

Like the organized cyber criminals, hackers for hire are in it for the financial gains. Unlike crime families, these hackers render their services to the highest bidder on a project-by-project basis.

Some hackers work alone, plying their trade in the underground economy. The more daring ones offer services on the Internet and make hacking as easy as online shopping. These sites typically grew out of offering mobile phone jail-breaking services for Xbox, iOS devices, etc., but later expanded their services to include botnets for hire or even targeted attack hacking. The website in Figure 2.4 specializes in a list of hacking services.

These types of services expand the realm of possibilities of hacking to the common folk. You don't need to have the expertise to hack, rent a SPAM engine, or launch a DDoS attack. You just need a reason and some cash. The *Wall Street Journal* reported a story in January 2012

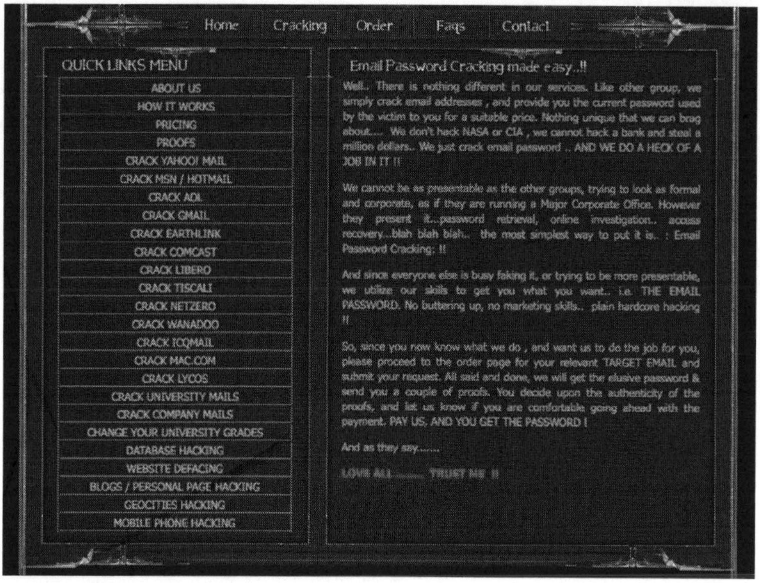

Figure 2.4 A website offering e-mail password hacking.

about a Kuwaiti billionaire, Bassam Alghanim, who found his personal e-mail, finances, and healthcare information being posted on the Internet for public viewing.[20] After some investigation, it was alleged that his brother hired hackers from China to break into Mr. Alghanim's e-mail for US$400. The motive behind hiring the hackers was rooted in a financial feud over the division of assets between the brothers.

2.6.2 Hackers for Hire and the Cloud

The cloud provides unlimited compute power to these hackers. Much like their counterpart, the hacktivists, hackers for hire leverage the cloud to launch attacks, host their systems, develop their tools, etc. Some cloud providers provide free trials and accounts, which only requires e-mail verification. The most common hacker-for-hire cloud break-in would be going after public e-mail accounts. Other prime targets include social networking sites, data storage providers, cloud-based document management systems, and contact management systems—basically, any data in the cloud that are desirable enough for someone to pay a hacker to retrieve.

2.6.3 Hackers for Hire and Mobility

The threat vector here for enterprises is not significant. Mobile hacking incidents to steal personal data, such as photos, e-mail, and text messages, are mainly targeted at celebrities. Here are some of the techniques used to compromise mobile phones:

- Password guessing/cracking: Due to the fact that most people use similar passwords for their social networking sites as well as their e-mails and other online applications, guessing or cracking one password may payoff in all other areas. Hackers target common sites like Twitter or Facebook to obtain passwords by guessing, running an intelligent password cracking engine, or answering the "forgot password" series of questions. Once they obtain the password to one account, they gain access to others.
- Social engineering: A determined hacker could obtain a cell phone carrier's administrative console through social engineering. This happened with T-Mobile and Paris Hilton.[21]

Hackers for hire could exploit this method, though most carriers have ramped up their security since the incident.

- Malware: Hackers can send targeted links for malware downloads to their victims to plant a spyware that enables remote access or data exfiltration.
- Physical access: Theft and shoulder browsing could easily compromise the typical four-digit lock code on phones.

For the enterprise, some executives may be targeted, and that may compromise company secret as well as personal data. The likelihood, however, is low.

2.6.4 Hackers for Hire and Security

The exposure from this group is mainly targeted at password cracking and social engineering. The following guidelines should provide a reasonable defense to these threats:

1. Improved authentication: Passwords have been the bane of security professionals but a necessary evil. I'm an advocate for adaptive authentication where you combine a strong password with a one-time password that is sent to the end user's mobile phone via text, e-mail, or voicemail. Better yet, the adaptive authentication system should keep track of the devices that it has seen before so as not to prompt for the second factor when the end user is coming from a device that's been dual authenticated. This provides usability with security. Password awareness needs to be a focus as well. Education needs to be provided to users to create hard-to-guess passwords that are difficult to crack by automated systems.

2. Security awareness: Forcing your user community to do a 2-hour computer-based training once a year is not security awareness, but rather an audit check box at best. Awareness has to be creative, ongoing, and relevant to be effective. Four key groups to focus most of your awareness dollars on are customer-facing support, senior executives, finance, and administrators with privileged access.

2.7 Insider Threat

Insiders can come from any one of the other groups. Hacktivists could exist within your company and have loyalties to a cause above their commitments to their day job. An organized criminal group might succeed in recruiting agents within your company by way of incentives or threats. A nation-state could easily recruit, train, and plant key informants and agents within your company if you are in the defense, key infrastructure, or government arenas. Your e-mail administrators may moonlight as hackers for hire, since they are experts in their domains. Insiders are not only limited to your employees, but nonemployees you let into your environment for business reasons:

- Offshore contractors or employees: They typically come from third world economies where labor is cheaper, but that also means the cost of buying their cooperation is lower.
- Outsourcers: Similar to offshore employees, outsourcers have access to your key systems and valuable information assets without you having full knowledge or control over their security and hiring practices.
- Contractors and consultants: These nonemployees have short- or long-term access to your systems and are typically hired for their expertise.
- Partners: Some companies open up limited access to foster symbiotic relationships. These channels are considered trusted, but you have little visibility into your partner organization's employees.

The point here is that insider threats are present and very difficult to detect because they have authorized access and pertinent knowledge of your systems and data. They also can cause the most significant harm. With that said, the 2012 Verizon "Data Breach Investigations Report" shows that the number of insider and partner breaches combined is still relatively low—less than 5% (Figure 2.5).

The key defenses against insider attacks are as follows:

- Build an anomalous-based detection system: This is easier said than done, but it is imperative that we rely solely on signature-based detection and focus on solutions that can flag variances in behavior.

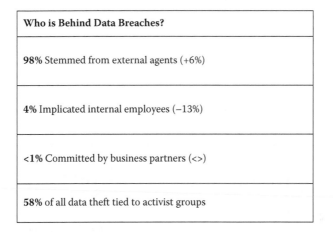

Who is Behind Data Breaches?
98% Stemmed from external agents (+6%)
4% Implicated internal employees (−13%)
<1% Committed by business partners (<>)
58% of all data theft tied to activist groups

Figure 2.5 Verizon™ DBIR report on threat agents. (From Verizon, "Data Breach Investigations Report 2012," accessed June 28, 2012, http://www.verizonbusiness.com/resources/reports/rp_data-breach-investigations-report-2012_en_xg.pdf.)

- Partner, offshore, and outsourcing personnel access and screening: Most public companies have employee screening as a normal hiring process. This is prevalent in the United States, where we have decent data about our citizens. When we look at other countries, background and credit checks are not readily available. Be cognizant about outsourcing and offshoring activities within your enterprise. Get involved in these projects and push for transparency in employee screening practices. Establish rigid and auditable access through gateway technologies so as to limit unfettered network access and provide a choke point for entry. Ask for the right to audit and enforce a periodic assessment to test their security posture. Conduct awareness programs that extend to these employees by collaborating with your outsourcer vendors and partners.

References

1. Stacy Cowley. An inside view of LulzSec's hacking rampage, CNNMoneyTech. Accessed June 28, 2012, http://money.cnn.com/2012/02/29/technology/cloudflare_lulzsec/index.htm.
2. Identity Theft Resource Center. 2011 ITRC breach report key findings. Accessed June 28, 2012, http://www.idtheftcenter.org/artman2/publish/headlines/Breaches_2011.shtml.

3. Symantec Corporation. The shocking scale of cybercrime. Accessed June 28, 2012, http://uk.norton.com/cybercrimereport/promo.

4. Ponemon Institute. Second annual cost of cybercrime study. Accessed June 28, 2012, http://www.arcsight.com/collateral/whitepapers/2011_Cost_of_Cyber_Crime_Study_August.pdf.

5. Stephen McCombie, Josef Pieprzyk, and Paul Watters. Cybercrime attribution: An Eastern European case study. Accessed June 28, 2012, http://ro.ecu.edu.au/adf/66/.

6. Jarrod Rifkind. Cybercrime in Russia. Center for Strategic and International Studies. Accessed June 28, 2012, http://csis.org/blog/cybercrime-russia.

7. Cisco. Cisco 2011 annual security report. Accessed June 28, 2012, http://www.cisco.com/en/US/prod/collateral/vpndevc/secu¬rity_annual_report_2011.pdf.

8. Verizon. 2011 data breach investigations report. Accessed June 28, 2012, http://www.verizonbusiness.com/us/Products/security/dbir/.

9. Eric Chien. Motivations of recent Android malware. Symantec Corporation. Accessed June 28, 2012, http://www.symantec.com/content/en/us/enterprise/media/security_response/whitepapers/motivations_of_recent_android_malware.pdf? om_ext_cid=biz_socmed_twitter_facebook_marketwire_linkedin_2011Oct__androidmalwarewhitepaper.

10. Jeremy Kirk. Apple developing fixes for iOS vulnerabilities. Accessed June 28, 2012, http://www.computerworld.com/s/article/9218233/Apple_developing_fixes_ for_dangerous_iOS_vulnerabilities.

11. John D. Sutter. iPhone bug could let hackers steal photos, contacts, and send texts. CNN. Accessed June 28, 2012, http://articles.cnn.com/2011-11-08/tech/tech_mobile_apple-ios-bug-apps_1_apple-s-app-store-apple-app-store-ios?_s=PM:TECH.

12. Ericsson. Ericsson money services bring connected mobile money to Europe. Accessed June 28, 2012, http://www.ericsson.com/news/110608_money_24 4188810_c.

13. Alex Wawro. Protect yourself from DNSChanger. *PCWorld*. Accessed June 28, 2012, http://www.pcworld.com/article/255137/protect_your¬self_from_dnschanger.html.

14. U.S. Department of Justice. Department of Justice takes action to disable international botnet. Accessed June 28, 2012, http://www.justice.gov/opa/pr/2011/April/11-crm-466.html.

15. Bryan Krekel. Capability of the People's Republic of China to conduct cyber warfare and computer network exploitation. U.S.-China Economic and Security Review Commission. Accessed June 28, 2012, http://www.uscc.gov/researchpapers/2009/NorthropGrumman_PRC_Cyber_Paper_FINAL_Approved%20Repor_16Oct2009.pdf.

16. Ashlee Vance. China wrests supercomputer title from the U.S. *New York Times*. Accessed June 28, 2012, http://www.nytimes.com/2010/10/28/technology/28compute.html.

17. BBC. Cyber-attack on BBC leads to suspicion of Iran's involvement. Accessed June 28, 2012, http://www.bbc.co.uk/news/technology-17365416.
18. India/Bangladesh cyberwar moves to a new level. *Infosecurity Magazine.* Accessed June 28, 2012, http://www.infosecurity-magazine.com/view/24328/indiabangladesh-cyberwar-moves-to-a-new-level/.
19. Department of Homeland Security. Office of Cybersecurity and Communications. Accessed June 28, 2012, http://www.dhs.gov/xabout/structure/gc_11852024 75883.shtm.
20. Cassell Bryan-Low. Hackers-for-hire are easy to find. *Wall Street Journal.* Accessed June 28, 2012, http://online.wsj.com/article/SB100014240529 70203471004577145140543496380.html.
21. Kevin Poulsen. Hacker penetrates T-Mobile systems. SecurityFocus. Accessed June 28, 2012, http://www.securityfocus.com/news/10271.

PART II

DECONSTRUCTING CLOUD SECURITY

Cloud has become a nebulous term due to its overusage and complexity. Marketing departments all across the IT world are branding cloud to cash in on the buzz. Microsoft Cloud Services is different from Apple's iCloud. Amazon Elastic Compute Cloud is not equivalent to Verizon Cloud Computing Program. How do you decide from the plethora of cloud services to choose from? On the private cloud side, you are faced with a forked road of deciding between the choice of enterprise cloud solutions such as VMWare, Xen, Hyper-V, etc. Every major vendor has a solution for orchestration and self-provisioning. Virtualization options are available at every layer: compute, network, storage, security, and endpoints. Cloud is turning out to be a cacophony of components that requires a trained ear to filter through the noise to find the right solution set in a sea of options.

As a security practitioner, understanding these differences is fundamental to building a viable security framework for your company's adoption or implementation of cloud. We believe that it is imperative that you have a high-level understanding of the general cloud components before diving into the security issues within each layer (which we will do in the next section). In this section, we will provide the building blocks needed to discuss cloud security. We start by asking the most basic question: Just because everyone is doing cloud, does it mean you have to? What are the advantages of embracing cloud technologies? What are important factors to consider?

By the end of this section, we hope that you can walk into any cloud discussions, understand the nuances of various cloud deployments, and make sound decisions on how to best secure your use of cloud.

3

Cloud Dialogues

3.1 Point of Cloud

As a security practitioner, you will be pulled into meetings where cloud discussions are going on. The CIO and your peers will ask you for your input on the direction to take. Security concerns have been a major barrier to public cloud adoption. Private cloud implementations require an update on existing security models. In addition to that, the economic climate has also put IT on the hot seat to deliver technology cheaper, faster, and better. Cloud has the potential to deliver on all three fronts, thus further increasing these conversations within the enterprise. Regardless of the hype, cloud is a reality to most businesses today and holds promise for the future. However, it is important to note that all things cloud are not created equal. As a practitioner, you need to be able to decode cloud-speak and translate that to your own challenges in order to add value to the discussions surrounding cloud. You need to know what the key benefits are so you can weigh them against risks and costs. The cloud dialogue revolves around the following topics (in varying degrees, depending on cloud deployment and service models):

- Capability: Cloud computing is able to extend your capabilities beyond what your current infrastructure can do today.
- Financials: There are avenues of savings attainable by cloud strategies that do not compromise functionality or performance.
- Agility: The cloud models provide the speed and flexibility needed by enterprises to serve the new economy.
- Security: There are significant implications to controlling confidentiality, availability, and integrity in the cloud.

- Licensing: Existing software licensing models are playing catch-up to cloud, and choosing the wrong license model could severely impact deployment decisions.
- Execution: With the variety of deployment and service models, cloud decision makers have to bridge their current environment with the future state architecture.

3.2 Capability

Your business units or corporate departments will come to IT with a project to replace an existing function or venture into a new capability by subscribing to a software as a service (SaaS) provider. This is because the business model of offering mature technology in a specific function at a near-zero ramp-up time is possible with cloud. The kicker, of course, is that it can do what you do and more for less than your capital and operational expense of hosting it in-house. You do not even have to "staff up" to maintain the software or deal with its outages. It is no wonder that SaaS growth was on track for $12.1 billion for 2011[1] according to a recent Gartner article.

On the infrastructure side, cloud can provide auto-provisioning, scale, uptime, bandwidth, and geographic expansion in much less time than it takes to build or migrate a single data center. There are nuances and limitations, which we will discuss later, but the basic capabilities to run high-production transactions globally on public clouds are a proven fact. Case in point, Netflix runs its core business entirely on Amazon Web Services (AWS). Many new companies that have not invested in physical data centers are looking to start in the cloud.

Your software developers will drive the case for platform as a service (PaaS). Capabilities here include the ability for improved development workflow, use of common models and reusable components, cross-domain monitoring, and rapid provisioning. Your heads of development will be banging on IT's door, if they have not already, to leverage the capabilities provided by public PaaS and possibly private PaaS implementations.

3.3 Financials

There are viable cost reasons to look at cloud options. Cloud gives us the ability to save in these ways:

- Not paying for what you don't use: Our data centers are sized for peaks as opposed to average. Our systems run at below-average capacity most of the time because we need to have the ability to handle high-traffic periods. In most cloud deployments, metered billing can be negotiated where billing occurs for the level of usage. Some companies may only leverage cloud for bursting instead of sizing their own implementation for peak. They size it for average and burst into the cloud when needed. Other companies will turn off services manually to cut down operational cost when they see that demand is not as they expected. When you provision your own data center, your cost of operations is not as flexible.

- Minimal upfront investment: As opposed to putting up the capital outlay to build a data center, subscription to a public or community cloud model may not only enable capital expenditure savings, but cut down deployment costs, which also add up to significant savings in labor, expertise, and liability.

- Low-cost option for disaster recovery (DR): The cost of standing up and maintaining a separate data center for the purposes of DR could be greatly reduced by embracing the cloud model. This option also provides a stepwise familiarity with using the cloud without affecting production or key business processes. Many companies have or are moving down this path to lower operational costs.

- Low-cost option for nonproduction environments: Similar to DR, development and certain preproduction environments are great candidates for the cloud due to looser availability and security requirements around these systems. Servers could be repurposed for production, saving the expense of buying new hardware.

- Reduce cost of IT resources: Depending on the cloud services chosen, significant savings can be obtained by not having to staff for functions that have moved to the cloud. Your enterprise may also benefit from the level of expertise that is covered by the price of the service.

Return on investment (ROI) has always been touted as one of the greatest benefits of cloud. There is a lot of truth in that, provided you make the right decisions along the way. Cloud can get very expensive if you botch your initial contract negotiations and underestimate the volume of your use cases. Licensing is complex in cloud, as software vendors are playing catch-up to the cloud revolution. A mismanagement of software licensing could lead to unpredictable costs. Another bane for cost reduction in cloud is customization. Cloud is about economy of scale, and customization breaks the optimization gain through orchestration of common objects. Cloud vendors will either not allow a high number of customizations or charge you a hefty price for them. Good planning, well-negotiated contracts, and meticulous execution will assure you of a good ROI.

3.4 Agility

Agility is the by-product of speed and elasticity. The choice for public clouds provides companies with the option of not having to build their own infrastructure, platform, or software. The ease and speed of deployment are probably the most appealing features of cloud computing, especially when you contrast the time, effort, expertise, and risk of standing up your own data centers and services. Companies know that going to market in today's fast-paced consumer world is a defining advantage. The mobility generation is used to downloading its apps right away and using them. Your new-generation development team expects the same. It wants to develop and push applications to the cloud instantaneously. Your next-generation product development geniuses want shorter cycles between ideation and production. Even your forward-thinking IT staff will wonder why auto-provisioning is not inherent in your infrastructure. As noted in the first chapter, the world as we know it has moved forward and agility in IT is fast becoming a necessity, not a luxury.

Cloud technologies provide unparalleled speed in deploying new capabilities. SaaS providers have ready-made applications that will only take weeks to go from zero to production. Additionally, the flexibility of scale is also built into the SaaS offering without having to refit your entire IT infrastructure.

The same goes for PaaS, where workflows and environments up to deploying apps to production can be done in speeds unparalleled to those of the old software development life cycle. Once again, scale is not an issue for most PaaS providers.

Infrastructure as a service (IaaS) also holds the same level of speed and flexibility. Provisioning new servers or environments is a matter of accessing the management interface, selecting your options, and hitting go. The behind-the-scenes orchestration is what sets cloud apart from old IT. A public cloud IaaS offering has to provide the self-provisioning capability to be called cloud. Otherwise, it would be no different than a hosting facility that offers managed infrastructure. The same goes for the enterprise; without orchestration and elasticity, you only have a virtualized environment, not a private cloud.

3.5 Security

Public cloud service providers entered the market with scale, cost, and functionality being key drivers, but many of them are aware of the increasing need for getting their security act together to court businesses that are highly regulated around customer privacy. In Parts III and IV of the book, we will discuss implementation strategies to secure private and public cloud. In this segment, let us explore the poignant issues around cloud adoption and information security.

Security has been often quoted as being the biggest barrier to migrating production to the public cloud. This is not entirely true but has merits worth exploring. Let's go ahead and break down some of the major concerns:

- Data assurance: The challenge here is for cloud players to provide reasonable assurances for data protection in their multitenant environment. This is especially difficult for industry silos that have high regulatory requirements around nonpublic personal information (NPPI). Cloud providers are playing catch-up in this space. However, there are viable solutions for encrypting data as well as the entire virtual stack in the cloud, while keeping key management in-house. The maturation of cloud encryption solutions and the ease of implementation will drive down the data assurance concerns.

- State of compliance: Government, financial, healthcare, retail, and other similar industry silos have significant NPPI concerns due to privacy regulations and breach implications. Correspondingly, these industries also have high levels of compliance and auditing activities. The audit reviews go through numerous security domains, from physical security to identity management to retention policies. Certification is required in certain cases. A majority of cloud providers are ill-equipped to handle the rigor that comes with these audits. Additionally, these controls vary from tenant to tenant and go against the one-size-fits-all model of public cloud. Community clouds have sprung up as a possible solution for companies with higher compliance requirements. Community cloud providers cater to specific industries, and thus have the know-how and cost model to meet the needs required by that industry. Case in point is IBM's Federal Cloud that was built to service federal agencies that require Federal Information Security Management Act (FISMA) compliance.

- Control and visibility: Public cloud providers do not tend to expose the inner-workings of their environment to their tenants. They have the burden of balancing what they show you against the privacy of other tenants. Some cloud providers may integrate with your centralized operations toolkits using common monitoring protocols such as the Simple Network Management Protocol (SNMP), syslog, and flow traffic. Most will provide limited monitoring functions and views on the cloud console. This lack of visibility and control significantly affects the information security department's ability to identify and respond to threat events. To mitigate these limitations, risk transference mechanisms such as contracts and indemnity clauses have to be applied. Basically, trust the cloud provider to monitor and control your security posture and make it pay if it fails. Innovative companies are cropping up to fill this space and provide a security shim between the enterprise and the cloud. The shim can provide single sign-on, data validation, and security protection, and can even enforce security rules prior to the request reaching the provider. Others are blazing down the path of building an entire layer of abstraction that sits on top of the cloud provider, which brings with it full visibility and control while leveraging cheap computation in the public cloud. Community cloud providers may have a more palatable solution for visibility and control, but at a higher cost.

- Availability: As one of the fundamental tenets in information security, we are concerned about the overall uptime of the cloud provider and how it impacts our production environment. This concern stems partly from the lack of visibility and control. We are used to seeing and dealing with issues in our data centers. When we migrate to the cloud, we are dependent on service level agreements (SLAs) and contracts to ensure the availability of our systems. Uptime is definitely a core capability of cloud service providers (CSPs), and they have a strong commitment to ensure high availability. History has shown us that even the best CSPs suffer unexpected outages because we are dealing with a technology that is still relatively new. On April 21, 2011, Amazon's Web Services on the U.S.–East segment suffered service disruptions that continued for 4 days due a network change that spawned a negative chain reaction on Amazon's Elastic Block Store.[2] Companies who designed their systems to anticipate potential cloud outages either remained online or were down for a minimal number of hours. Thousands of other online sites on AWS were down for days. The key lesson here is that cloud infrastructures are highly complex and availability is not guaranteed, no matter how big the cloud players are. You have to anticipate and design for outages.

- Identity and access management: In the SaaS space, the prevalent method is for the CSP to provide a user management console through the standard administration portal to facilitate self-management by the customer. Other, more forward-thinking CSPs allow for authentication back to your Active

Directory (AD) or Lightweight Directory Access Protocol (LDAP) through the Security Assertion Markup Language (SAML). Other identity cloud providers have also stepped up to bridge the gap by providing an identity gateway between your AD and multiple SaaS providers, thus giving you cloud single sign-on. When surveying a cloud provider, make sure to understand its ability to support integrated identity management approaches. Implementation considerations for identity and access management will be discussed in later chapters.

While security is a major concern for cloud adoption, there are instances where going to cloud serves to benefit security. Selecting the right CSP will allow you to inherit its security posture from the get-go. Adopting a community cloud that understands the security and compliance needs of your industry may also expedite the improvements to your security stance and potentially lower your costs.

3.6 Licensing

Licensing is an area where careful consideration has to be given in a private or public cloud scenario. For private clouds, the choice of virtualization technology could significantly drive your cost due to the different price structures of each technology. Licensing models for virtualization are still evolving. You have to identify license bands depending on your requirements or use. In Microsoft's model, there are Data Center, Enterprise, and Standard editions. For VMWare, the terminology is the same for Enterprise and Standard, but the premium grade is called Enterprise Plus instead of Data Center. These grades offer different benefits, functions, and toolsets. Figure 3.1 shows an example of VMWare's different bands for vSphere 5.0.

VMWare used to charge by physical processor but is moving to a licensing model that restricts based on vRAM and vCPU. Furthermore, the bands restrict your ability for orchestration due to the toolset provided in each rung. Microsoft takes the approach of not charging for the virtualization software, but licensing on running instances (loading the OS into memory) (Figure 3.2).

The virtualization licensing models are adjusted over time to contend with Moore's law in the advancement processing power.

	Standard	Enterprise	Enterprise Plus
Entitlements per CPU license			
• vRAM entitlement	32 GB	64 GB	96 GB
• vCPU/VM	8 way	8 way	32 way
Features			
• Hypervisor	✓	✓	✓
• High availability	✓	✓	✓
• Data recovery	✓	✓	✓
• vMotion	✓	✓	✓
• Virtual serial port concentrator		✓	✓
• Hot add		✓	✓
• vShield zones		✓	✓
• Fault tolerance		✓	✓
• Storage APIs for array integration		✓	✓
• Storage vMotion		✓	✓
• Distributed resource scheduler & distributed power management		✓	✓
• Distributed switch			✓
• I/O controls (network and storage)			✓
• Host Profiles			✓
• **Auto Deploy***			✓
• **Policy-Driven Storage***			✓
• **Storage DRS***			✓
***New in vSphere 5.0**			

Figure 3.1   VMWare® license bands.

VMWare started out licensing by processors and cores, but as VM density increased per physical host, VMWare moved to a vRAM and vCPU approach to protect itself from diminished returns over time. Microsoft continues to focus on charging for its operating systems and enterprise applications rather than licensing on its virtualization platform. Other virtualization players use different models. It is important

Product	Maximum permitted running instances in a virtual OSE per license
Windows Server 2008 Standard	One
Windows Server 2008 Enterprise	Four
Windows Server 2008 Datacenter	Unlimited
Windows Server 2008 for Itanium Based Systems	Unlimited
Windows Web Server 2008	One*

Figure 3.2   Microsoft® license bands.

for you to understand the nature of your environment and the cost model you prefer before embarking on a virtualization platform.

Once you sort out your licensing needs for the VM and OS, you have the distinct pleasure of wading through the complexities of licensing applications that run on your VMs. Software companies are struggling to come up with licensing strategy that keeps them profitable while providing agility and flexibility to service the on-demand model of cloud infrastructures. Most software companies cannot distinguish between a virtual OS and a physical OS, and thus they cannot price these two licenses differently. In those cases, you pay traditional licensing fees of per server or per device charges. Due to the elasticity of cloud, you can spike your server count up to five times your average to meet market demands. If the traditional license models tabulate per device count for your peak and not your average, you may end up being out of compliance with your license agreements or end up paying penalties during the true-up process.

Other applications are VM-aware and put restrictions on the environment on which you run it. One of the most notorious examples of this is Oracle's licensing as it pertains to VMs.

For AMD and Intel processors, Oracle charges the licensing rights of the database multiplied by the number of physical cores, multiplied by the number of processors, and finally multiplied by 0.5. Oracle does not charge or limit the running instances of the databases you want to instantiate on the VM cluster. Let me illustrate with an example. If the price of an Oracle 11g database is $50K and you run 20 Oracle instances in a cluster of 10 physical servers with 2 cores of quad processors, you will end up paying $50K * 10 physical servers * 2 cores * 4 processors * 0.5 = $2M. Here's how Oracle licensing affects your VM physical segmentation design. If you reserve 2 out of your 10 servers to run the 20 instances of Oracle, then your licensing fee becomes $50K * 2 physical servers * 2 cores * 4 processors * 0.5 = $400K. By making a slight alteration to your environment, you save $1.6M in licensing fees. This is not exactly ideal for your VM clustering design and ease of administration, but the licensing model could essentially change the layout of your private cloud implementation.

3.7 Service Level Agreements

When considering public clouds, it is paramount to examine their service level agreements (SLAs) to ensure that your fundamental business needs are met to your requirements. The following are the key SLA components to consider:

- Uptime: The availability of your business is now dependent on your cloud provider. You need to understand its uptime guarantee, service failure notification, and service credits in the event of an outage. Some cloud providers may guarantee 100% uptime but place a cap on your service credits for outages. Others may offer a lower uptime in addition to capping your service credits. You also need to examine your provider's legal definitions for outages. Not being diligent with uptime SLA may result in a cloud outage that translates to lost revenues that cannot be recouped due to SLA stipulations.
- Network performance: Just because a service is up does not mean it is satisfactory. Again, definitions are important because you may be guaranteed uptime, but if the network performance is unacceptable, you will still have loss revenue due to unhappy customers. You need to understand and define acceptable levels of network performance and ensure that they are stipulated in your SLA.
- Maintenance windows and change management: Scheduled outages can be inside or outside the purview of uptime SLAs. You need to clarify if maintenance windows are included or excluded in the uptime guarantee. Furthermore, you need to understand the conditions and stipulations around a CSP's maintenance windows so that you can meet your customer's expectations. You may also want to understand the extent of transparency a CSP provides for changes made to environments that affect your portion of its cloud.
  - What notifications are provided to you in the event of changes done during the maintenance windows?
  - What is its general rollback procedure if things do not go as planned?
- Unfortunately, most CSPs do not provide an adequate level of transparency to their inner workings.

- Response times and incident management: There are various severity levels to production issues. You need to ensure that response times for each of these severity levels are clearly specified. You also need to have a clear process for escalations, exception handling, and notification. From a security perspective, you need to understand the terms in which you will be notified of a security breach. You need to confirm how you participate in the Computer Security Incident Response Team (CSIRT). You have to establish SLAs around identification, containment, recovery, and remediation.
- Data guarantees: Information is the lifeblood of your production systems. You need to be clear about all the SLAs surrounding data availability, integrity, privacy, security, and performance.
  - Does your uptime SLA cover data access and availability?
  - How and where are your data replicated or backed up?
  - Do you have any restrictions on which country your data can reside in?
  - What encryption capabilities will the CSP provide for your data?
  - Which portion of the data life cycle will be encrypted?
  - If there's encryption, are the key management procedures acceptable? These are just the tip of the iceberg.

You have to systematically vet out service levels around data protection, governance, and use.

From the private cloud perspective, you may be required to provide SLAs to your internal customers. Consider the same factors above and design controls and metrics to report on the core SLA components.

References

1. Christy Pettey. Gartner says North America to account for 64 percent of SaaS revenue in 2011 Gartner. Accessed June 28, 2012, http://www.gartner.com/it/page.jsp?id=1791514.
2. Amazon Web Services. Summary of the Amazon EC2 and Amazon RDS service disruption in the US East Region. Accessed June 28, 2012, http://aws.amazon.com/message/65648/.

PART III
SECURING
PRIVATE CLOUD
COMPUTING

This section provides practical steps for securing your cloud infrastructure. We will start by talking about private clouds because the principles are more familiar and are extensions of your current security practice. Most enterprises are experimenting with the idea of converting their data centers to cloud models. Their first foray is typically capitalizing on server virtualization. While this is not true private cloud, it is the foundation of any private cloud infrastructure. The evolution of server virtualization to multitenancy, agility, elasticity, and utility is a major hurdle that most of us are facing today. Those of us who choose to do it within our control boundaries are faced with having to meet these technological advancements with old and new security measures.

The chapters in this section will systematically cover each one of the following security considerations in greater detail to provide you with pragmatic steps for addressing your private cloud security posture

- Physical and logical segmentation: Cloud technologies are built around the premise of leveraging pooled resources. Physical segmentation erodes the economy of scale but increases the availability and security of applicable segments. The proper use of logical segmentation at the network, hypervisor, and storage layers could be used to balance the equation between scale and security.

- Orchestration and cloud administration: One of the key differentiators of cloud computing versus the traditional model. Orchestration facilitates self-service computing, which is another tenet of cloud computing. The security context has to be designed into the orchestration policies and processes. Cloud administration is the portal used to build, run, and monitor the private cloud implementation. This might also be the same portal as the orchestration management console.

- Encryption services: Regulated data sets such as credit card numbers, nonpublic personal information, etc., may require encryption. Understanding encryption technologies available within cloud architectures is instrumental to delivering a holistic solution that does not interfere with function and performance. The life cycle of managing keys is also a factor in designing encryption services.

- Threat intelligence: This consideration addresses the coalescing of threat data into a Security Information Event Manager (SIEM) and applying the right filter to generate intelligent triggers that can be acted upon. With cloud, you have the option of scraping system and network level data from the hypervisor in addition to your existing abilities of agent-based and network-based detection.

- Identity management: Private cloud will open up a self-service interface to different parts of the organization. You need to review the role-based access control capabilities of the cloud solution to ensure entitlements and role management. Additionally, you will also have to consider identity governance issues with the proliferation of systems and application in the new cloud model. Additionally, you might want to consider public cloud extensions in your identity governance design.

4

SEGMENTATION AND THE PRIVATE CLOUD

4.1 Physical and Logical Segmentation

The benefits and hype around cloud computing could compel your business and IT executives to revamp your existing environment. Your security posture is probably a mishmash of standards and controls due to organic growth and neglect over the years. The move to private cloud may be an opportunity for rearchitecting your security framework from the ground up.

Ironically, the physical layer is fundamental to designing a sound virtual environment. From a security perspective, you have to consider how you want to physically segment your network. Cloud computing pushes the economy of scale, and that is typically achieved by setting up a single virtual cluster for all your computing needs. However, security requirements might dictate a different agenda of pooling your computing and storage resources. It might also drive your decision making around firewall technology, and where to draw the physical fences versus virtual ones.

The production environment is where you run live systems that generate revenue for your company. Preproduction is where you test your systems prior to migration to production. This is typically where your staging, quality assurance, and possibly testing environments are. Development is where you build these systems. Enterprise is for your back-office systems, such as e-mails, finance, billing, etc. Many organizations have different business units that will further segment your environments down the lines of business. Migrating to private cloud would minimally change your environment setup.

These are some of the key factors that will affect your decision around segmentation:

- Environment requirements: In the private cloud design, the decision to physically or logically segregate your various production and nonproduction environments has cost and functional implications. If you choose to form physical separation for each environment down the network, server, and storage stack, you will de-leverage the advantage of cloud computing entirely. Knowing how to use physical versus logical separation will ensure that you maximize your elasticity and scalability without compromising your security posture.
- Fault-tolerance requirements: Physical separation ensures that revisions or deficiencies in core cloud infrastructure do not impact the entire environment and allows for one cluster to fall back on a different physical cluster.
- Compliance requirements: Depending on your industry silo, you may have varying degrees of scrutiny from regulatory bodies. Additionally, financial regulators have also mandated that downstream third parties that handle confidential data be held to the same standards. Compliance requirements are typically targeted at specific sets of systems. The Sarbanes-Oxley Act (SOX), Payment Card Industry (PCI), and ISO 27001/2 have the concept of drawing a boundary around in-scope versus out-of-scope systems. In your private cloud implementation, segmentation rules might apply around systems that have high compliance requirements. A more stringent set of security policies and control should apply to this segment. This may impact your decision around physical versus logical segmentation.
- Licensing requirements: As noted in Chapter 2, licensing models may significantly affect the cost of your cloud deployment. In the Oracle case, the licensing centered on physical cores and processors. Physically separating a cluster to only host Oracle databases may result in savings of millions.

4.2 Physical Segmentation

Segmentation in traditional models was done using the following methods:

- Physical servers

- Physical network devices
- Physical firewalls

Figure 4.1 illustrates the traditional lines of segmentation using physical interfaces and hardware.

Physical segmentation has the inherent benefit of isolation. Separating environments physically ensures that the lack of security controls in one environment does not affect the other. This might also translate into savings where you choose to invest a majority of security tools in the high-risk environment, as opposed to spreading your cost to inoculate the entire environment. Segmentation allows you to treat each area in accordance with its control requirements. In addition to security, fault tolerance is also a benefit to physical segmentation. Networking, server, or storage area network (SAN) issues in nonproduction will have no bearing on production. The main issue with physical separation is the cost associated with buying hardware, carving out rack space, and the consumption of power and cooling of these separated environments. Physical separation will also prevent the economy-of-scale, orchestration, and fault tolerance automations that are available in virtualization

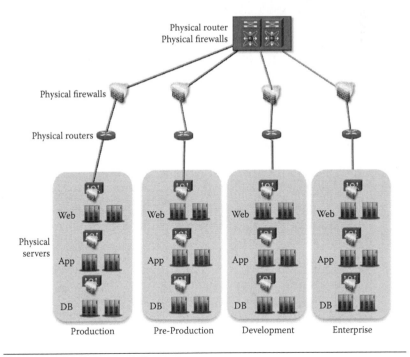

Figure 4.1   Physical segmentation.

technologies. The evolution of private cloud computing requires using a combination of physical and virtual segmentation technologies to achieve the fine balance of maximizing the advantages of virtualization while maintaining an acceptable security posture.

4.3 Physical and Virtual Segmentation

The use of segmentation is fundamental to ensuring availability and drawing security boundaries. With the advent of cloud and virtualization, segregation can be done with both physical and virtual elements:

- Hypervisor clusters: Physical hypervisor hosts that are grouped together to form compute pools for the virtualized infrastructure. Separate physical clusters can be dedicated to different environments. If the production environment is physically separated from the nonproduction environment at the server layer, then there cannot be sharing of computer resources between these two environments.
- Virtual firewalls: There are three types of virtual firewalls:
  - Virtual firewall instance: Next-generation firewall vendors have the ability to instantiate separate virtual firewall instances from a single physical device. These virtual firewalls have their own stand-alone configuration, interfaces, and security policies. These firewalls are advantageous because they do not consume or depend on the hypervisor cluster for computing or performance. They are sized exactly to do firewall functions and typically have state-of-the art firewall technologies.
  - Virtual firewall appliance: There are software-based firewall instances that run on virtual machines. This firewall has no physical instance and draws computing and memory power from the hypervisor. This is akin to the old firewall software that ran on physical machines with operating systems. The firewall appliance is built to run on virtual machines.
  - Hypervisor-based firewalls: There are a handful of vendors that play in this space today because they have to be given rights within the hypervisor through application programming interfaces (APIs). The APIs are controlled by the

hypervisor vendors, and thus may only allow limited capabilities and visibility for firewalling functions. Hypervisor firewalls are also known to be rudimentary in their implementation compared to firewall instantiations or the virtual appliances. Being at the hypervisor level, these firewalls can be provisioned with the virtual templates, creating a consistent security context across the virtual environment. The hypervisor firewalls are designed to be virtualization aware, thus facilitating fluid virtual machine movements while maintaining the intended security context.

- Virtual switching: Similar to firewalls, there are three forms of virtual switches (Figure 4.2):
  - Virtual switches instantiated from the physical switch
  - Virtual switch appliance deployed on a virtual machine
  - Hypervisor-based switching

Decisions around segregation have a direct impact on your private cloud deployment. Furthermore, choosing the right segmentation technology to use, be it physical or virtual, will also have a downstream effect to the cost, adaptability, fault tolerance, and security of your implementation. Understanding your requirements is fundamental to deploying the right level of segmentation with the right tools.

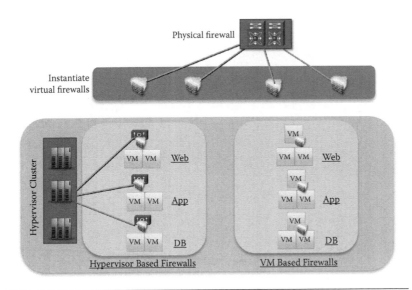

Figure 4.2   Three types of virtual firewalls.

Each business has different requirements, so there is no one-size-fits-all solution to the problem. To that end, we will outline different scenarios and present a reference diagram of segmentation to illustrate where segmentation can be done to achieve different desired goals.

4.4 Highly Optimized Segmentation Model

The reference model shown in Figure 4.3 is aligned to the primary goal of achieving the highest levels of cost savings and flexibility for your private cloud implementation.

The highly optimized model has its fair share of advantages versus disadvantages (Table 4.1). Each industry has varying thresholds for the different risks in each area. Companies that have high PCI compliance issues might want to consider carving out a separate physical hypervisor cluster for in-scope systems. If you run a lot of software that are licensed on physical cores, you may want to consider segregating physical clusters to just run these specific software. The general principle with virtualization and cloud technologies is that the more you segregate, the less optimized you are from a resource pooling and orchestration perspective.

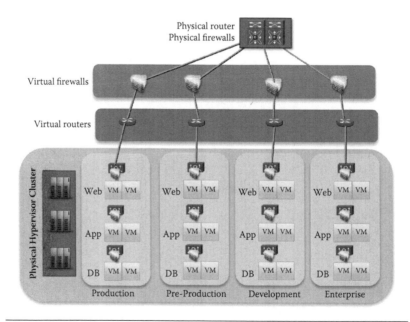

Figure 4.3 Highly optimized segmentation.

Table 4.1   Pros and Cons for Highly Optimized Segmentation Model

Description	• A single set of physical hypervisor clusters.
	• Minimal physical separation.
	• Segmentation is done via hypervisor policies, virtual switches, and hypervisor or virtually instantiated firewalls.
	• Separation is done by environments and tiered architecture.
	• This model can be extended to multiple tenants by extending the virtual firewalling schema to encapsulate an environment (not illustrated in Figure 4.3).
Advantages	• Provides the highest form of optimization and economy of scale by pooling all compute resources.
	• Lowers capital and operational cost of physical hardware by leveraging virtual firewalls and switching.
	• Speed in deployment and rapid provisioning due to a single pane of management and the lack of physical barriers.
	• Provides maximum elasticity due to the wide range of resource pools.
	• Ensures policy enforcement by integrating firewall policies with hypervisor policies. Also provides the fluid and consistent movement of security controls across virtual contexts.
	• Hypervisor firewalls provide visibility to inter-VM communication.
	• Simplifies orchestration by leveraging virtualized firewalling and switching.
Disadvantages	• Minimal fault tolerance for key infrastructure upgrades because the test environment runs on the same physical hypervisor cluster. Might want to consider building out a scaled-down but separate physical hypervisor cluster to simulate upgrades or vet issues prior to rolling it out on live environments. This may add a little overhead upfront but might be significant savings in issue avoidance.
	• A critical error or issue at the hypervisor could have a cascading effect on all environments due to the lack of physical separation.
	• Due to the common resource pool model, an issue in development could end up usurping the resources from production environments, creating performance or availability issues. Proper planning and configuration must be conducted to restrict resource allocation according to business requirements. The single hypervisor clustering creates misconfiguration risk exposures that may have far-reaching impacts.
	• There are known threats targeting out-of-date hypervisors that could compromise the integrity of all systems in all environments. This model is highly vulnerable to any threats targeting the hypervisor where the impact is not contained to a specific environment.
	• Hypervisor firewalls lack the capability and maturity of the other variants of virtual firewalls.

(continued)

Table 4.1   Pros and Cons for Highly Optimized Segmentation Model (continued)

Disadvantages	• Lack of segregation of duties. The VM administrator has the keys to the entire kingdom in every environment. With that said, a strict role-based, access control model can be implemented to mitigate this risk. Review of current IT organizational structure and segmented access to the administrative consoles for the hypervisor cluster is paramount to a sound security posture.
	• Compliance issues may prevail around segregation of production from nonproduction or nonpublic personal information (NPPI) data from development and test data. Depending on the regulation and auditor, logical separation may evoke a higher level of scrutiny versus physical segregation. The PCI-DSS Virtualization Guidelines published in June 2011* state: "If any virtual component connected to (or hosted on) the hypervisor is in scope for PCI DSS, the hypervisor itself will always be in scope." The basic principle here is that any common component that is in scope for PCI-DSS implicates all environments running on that common component. The PCI-DSS Virtualization Council is not a supporter of mixing VMs with different trust levels. Depending on the qualified security assessor (QSA), you may have a significant scope creep to your PCI assessment. Our guidance here is to have position papers published for your logical segmentation and possibly run the segmentation designs through your QSA before implementing your private cloud infrastructure.
	• Licensing costs that are tied to physical processors and cores will be applied to your entire physical hypervisor cluster. As noted in an earlier discussion around Oracle® licensing, this may be a difference of millions of dollars for the same exact functionality.

* Virtualization Special Interest Group PCI Security Standards Council, "PCI Data Security Standards 2.0," accessed June 28, 2012, https://www.pcisecuritystandards.org/documents/Virtualization_InfoSupp_v2.pdf.

4.5 Production-Based Segmentation Model

This model focuses on keeping the production environment pristine and separate from the nonproduction environments while providing a sizable pooling of computation resources by only creating two pods (Figure 4.4 and Table 4.2).

4.6 Storage Segmentation Model

Physical separation also extends to the storage layer. In the highly optimized model, storage of production and nonproduction environments should exist on the same physical storage area network (SAN) system. You may have a number of different legacy storage solutions in your environment, ranging from network-attached storage (NAS)

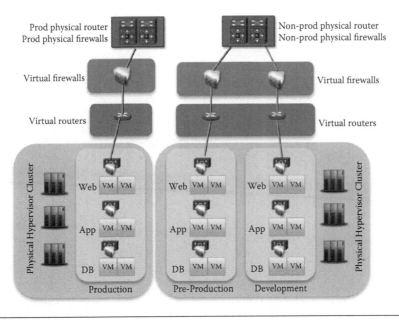

Figure 4.4 Production-based segmentation model.

to different SAN solutions. The private cloud initiative might be an opportunity to standardize on a single SAN architecture, but that is completely dependent on your situation. In the highly optimized segmentation model where there is only one physical hypervisor cluster, deploy a single SAN system to decrease capital and operational costs from a hardware and management perspective. In the production-based segregation model, create a separate physical SAN environment for the production hypervisor cluster. Logically segment your storage by separating logical unit numbers (LUNs).

Here are the general guidelines around SAN segregation for a multitenant environment (Figure 4.5):

- Allocate separate LUNs for the OS. Every VM can access the same OS LUN if they are part of the same tenant. Tenant separation at the data level has benefits when addressing compliance requirements for certain standards or certifications.
- Allocate separate data LUNs in different tiers. The rationale here is that different tiers have different input/output (I/O) requirements. You can use cheaper disks for low-I/O

Table 4.2 Pros and Cons for Production-Based Segmentation Model

Description	• Hard-line physical separation between production and nonproduction environments such as staging, testing, quality assurance, development, and even enterprise.
	• Physical segmentation is achieved by using physical hardware firewalls and switches. A separate physical hypervisor cluster is dedicated to the production environments. Virtual firewalls are used to separate the tiers between web, application, and databases. This model can be extended to a multitenant model by adding more virtual firewalls within the physical production cluster.
	• A separate set of physical firewalls, switches, and hypervisor cluster is dedicated to the nonproduction environments.
	• Storage should also be physically separate between the two physical clusters (not shown).
Advantages	• Critical errors or issues in the nonproduction hypervisor cluster will not have a cascading effect on the production environment.
	• Increases fault tolerance for key infrastructure upgrades because the test environment runs on a separate physical hypervisor cluster. Thorough testing for core upgrades can be done in the nonproduction environment before migrating to production. This provides a higher level of availability assurance.
	• Segregation of duties for production environments can be achieved by creating separate access to the hypervisor cluster's administrative interfaces.
	• Since all production environments runs on the same VM cluster, pooling and elasticity are still advantageous in this model.
	• Compliance requirements typically demand separation between production and nonproduction. This model has an end-to-end segregation between these two environments.
	• The use of hypervisor firewalls at the web, application, and database tiers provides policy enforcement by integrating firewall policies with hypervisor policies. This also provides the fluid and consistent movement of security controls across virtual contexts within the production environment.
	• Prevents hypervisor-based attacks from moving from a lax security zone (in the nonproduction environment) to the production environment.
Disadvantages	• Higher capital and operational expenditure on hardware for an additional set of physical firewalls, switches, and hypervisor cluster.
	• Due to the common resource pools, a peak in one portion of the VM cluster may have a cascading impact on other parts of the production environment. Proper planning is necessary to ensure that pool limitations are segmented based on needs. Define strict rules around your pooling and ensure that your resource pool has room for bursting.

(continued)

Table 4.2   Pros and Cons for Production-Based Segmentation Model (continued)

Disadvantages	• While this model addresses the compliance issue of segregating production from nonproduction, the scope of the audit might still extend to all of production as opposed to a subset of systems. The burden of proof will fall on you to demonstrate that the logical separation employed is adequate to contain the compliance requirements to a limited set of servers. Follow the same guidance above about establishing position papers around your logical segregation and getting them vetted by your auditors.
	• Licensing costs that are tied to physical processors and cores will be applied to your entire production physical hypervisor cluster. You may have considerable savings because the nonproduction physical clusters are no longer included. However, further physical segmentation within production might be required to address licensing restrictions. You have to weigh the costs accordingly and consider your growth trajectory for the use of these types of licenses.

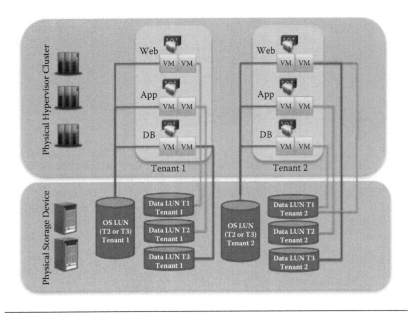

Figure 4.5   Storage segmentation model.

systems, thus improving your ROI. Furthermore, using fast disks for high-I/O tiers will also improve performance and user experience.

• If you have strong compliance requirements, there are options to purchase storage with hardware encryption. Consider this if there is a requirement to encrypt all your data.

5

ORCHESTRATION AND CLOUD MANAGEMENT

5.1 What Is Orchestration?

Orchestration, like cloud computing, is a word that means different things to different people. Here is what we mean when we use the term *orchestration*:

- Definition: Automation of network, computation, and data layers to form cohesive workflows that provide self-service functionality to the enterprise.
- Purpose: Abstract the technical layers and provide the business with speed, consistency, and efficiency when using IT services.
- Context: We will narrow the scope of our orchestration discussion to information security and private cloud computing in this chapter.

5.2 Benefits and Challenges

Orchestration is a fundamental principle to deploying private clouds due to the following benefits:

- Abstraction: Orchestration has to appear simple to the end user, but the underlying automation is anything but simple.
- Speed: Orchestration allows business users to choose IT services from a menu and have those services provisioned in short order. On the back end, these services are fulfilled by automating and coordinating the various interfaces across the IT stack in virtually real time.
- Consistency: Orchestration takes the human element out of the equation. Users can expect the same product every time at the same level of service.

- Cost efficiency: Orchestration significantly reduces the administrative overhead by automating interfaces between the network, computation, and data layers without human intervention. There is also savings in the cost of incidents and delays caused by human error. Additionally, orchestration also facilitates utility billing, which equates to users only paying for what they use. Orchestration puts control in the hands of end users, who in turn control their direct usage. This behavioral change is fundamental to accurately sizing the operational needs and costs of your data center.
- Standardization: This is a key benefit to information security. In order for automation to work, standards have to be established. Information security standards must be infused into the orchestration workflow to ensure the steady application of security controls every time.

Here are the challenges to orchestration:

- Customization: In order for orchestration to work, it has to be predictable. Customization is the bane of orchestration because it creates exceptions in an otherwise predictable workflow. That said, forcing the business to adopt a one-size-fits-all regiment would ultimately hurt the marketability of its products. A rigorous exercise of aligning IT to business is critical to formulating the limited menu option for IT services that are to be automated. The understanding is that cost of orchestration goes up with the number of customization.
- Complexity: Orchestration requires a series of complex interfaces to work together as a coherent unit. Depending on the legacy components in your environment, interfaces may not exist for the purposes of automation. Additionally, some vendors cannot, and possibly will not, collaborate with each other.
- Proliferation: The ease of deployment could lead to the proliferation of your orchestrated components. IT's ability to predict and control usage is now at the mercy of business users who can provision as many instances as they want or need.

The importance of planning for orchestration cannot be overemphasized to address the issue of customization. This begins with having a strong understanding of what business wants from IT. Since customization will be limited by having to offer a manageable selection of options, creating the initial set of service offerings must align to the majority of the business needs. Start by gathering and analyzing the plethora of requests IT has gotten over the past year. What is the typical server build? What flavors of OS, middleware, and database are being used? What are the usual performance and storage requirements? This may be a good opportunity to establish a standards board comprising key IT and business stakeholders. Oftentimes companies grow their IT haphazardly, and they end up supporting every flavor of OS and enterprise software. The licensing and operating costs are higher than necessary and support becomes untenable and expensive. Standardization can drive toward cost savings, lowered administrative overhead, reusable components, common interfaces, and speed to market. Exceptions will always exist but have to be kept to a minimum.

Orchestration is complex because of the lack of common standards across the major vendors. You have a choice of selecting a homogenous solution that covers the entire IT stack of network, computing, and storage or going with the play-nice-with-everyone solution. The homogenous solution is going to be easier to deploy due to the amount of control and testing the vendor and its set of partners have done to ensure that the entire solution set works as advertised. The issues are obvious in that you are limited by the capabilities of the vendor (and its partners), and there is a significant lock-in factor (the initial sunk costs plus the exit fee will be exorbitant). The heterogeneous option gives you the flexibility to build the best of breed, but you will have challenges with compatibility and seamless end-to-end functionality.

It is complicated enough to manage networks, computation, and data in their own separate layers. Tack on automation across these disciplines, and then multiply it by the level of complexity. Establishing clear business and IT requirements is the single most important step. Having a clear vision of what IT services you want to offer will drive your decisions around the orchestration management software, the cost models, and the performance and availability requirements, and vetting out incompatibilities across the IT stack and incorporating proof of concepts into your deployment will incrementally lower the complexity index of your solution.

Establishing clear expectations to your end users, incorporating proactive monitoring, analyzing usage trends, and enforcing standards can prevent uncontrolled proliferation of your cloud environment.

5.3 Information Security Considerations

Orchestration creates some unique advantages as well as challenges for information security practitioners. From a security perspective, the orchestration blueprint is a composite of a series of components that have to work well together in a secure fashion (Figure 5.1).

The following are areas of consideration for information security as it pertains to orchestration:

- Secure service delivery interface: Incorporate the appropriate controls by examining the end-to-end life cycle of the service to be provisioned.
- Secure resource delivery: Conduct a security design review across the automation process from an operational perspective.

Figure 5.1   Orchestration security.

- Secure orchestration management: The management interfaces for orchestration dictate the availability and security of your entire environment and must be properly secured.
- Security monitoring: Develop visibility of malicious or anomalous behavior during the orchestration process.

5.3.1 Secure Service Delivery Workflows

As noted earlier, orchestration starts with understanding the business need. The next step is to translate those business needs into an IT service catalog that will be the basis of your self-service offerings. You then convert these service offerings to infrastructure provisioning via orchestration workflows and capabilities.

Table 5.1 shows the security areas to focus on at the service delivery stage.

5.3.2 Secure Resource Delivery Automation

Orchestration begins with the user requesting an IT service from the portal and ends with coordination through the various IT layers to provision the requested service for the requestor. The orchestration engine centrally manages the end-to-end delivery of resources through application programming interfaces (APIs) that interact with all necessary components to provide the IT service requested on the self-service portal. As noted earlier, this solution could be heterogeneous where the orchestration console adopts an open model and works with myriad vendors. The other option is a homogenous solution that has a preestablished set of vendor ecosystems. Each solution has its pros and cons. Regardless of the option, the orchestration engine, at the minimum, has to build interfaces among the virtualization platform, the network components, the OS provisioning, and the storage layer. The more sophisticated orchestration engines will have connectors for billing systems, ticketing software, the application layer, security solutions, monitoring capabilities, and even bursting the internal cloud to the public domain.

Focus on the security areas shown in Table 5.2 when automating resource delivery.

Table 5.1   Security Considerations for Secure Service Delivery

FOCUS AREAS	SECURITY CONSIDERATIONS

Service catalog security	• The service catalog, in this context, is a set of IT services that you plan to offer to your users via the self-service cloud portal.
	• The service catalog contains various templates of IT services with variable compute, storage, and network elements.
	• Security requirements must be established for each layer of the template.
	  • Hardened OS layer: Require that operating systems within the template be configured to be secured by default.
	  • Endpoint security: Require that all VMs are provisioned with the right endpoint security agents, such as AV, DLP agent, etc.
	  • Appropriate network zoning: Require that IP allocation and dynamic firewall rules be added to the template to restrict the requested IT resources to their appropriate security context.
	  • Storage logical unit number (LUN) allocation: Require that the templates follow your secure LUN segmentation model.

Self-service cloud portal	• The self-service interface is a portal where end users request their auto-provisioned IT services. • Like any web portal, secure coding practices need to be employed here in accordance with Open Web Application Security Project (OWASP) standards. • Harden the web server and the OS. Ensure that regular patch management is conducted. • Limit access to the self-service portal to users who have a business need. If the portal needs to be accessed outside the enterprise, utilize a virtual private network (VPN). • Establish authentication requirements for access to the self-service portal. The recommendation here is to use your enterprise's Active Directory logon or its equivalent. • Identify and establish roles and determine entitlements for requesting IT services based on roles. • Establish approval workflows to ensure that appropriate checks and balances are inherent in the service request.
Utilization	• Orchestration puts control in the hands of users to provision IT services whenever they need. • From an availability perspective, the appropriate technical controls must be placed to govern the requests for IT services. A flurry of requests could maximize the load on the private cloud and potentially affect other business areas. • Options within the service catalog must have preestablished limitations. • Checks and balances must be incorporated in the design to ensure that the appropriate levels of allocation are granted without causing disruptions to other parts of the cloud ecosystem.

(continued)

Table 5.1   Security Considerations for Secure Service Delivery (continued)

FOCUS AREAS	SECURITY CONSIDERATIONS
Utilization	• Proper approval workflows and reviews must be embedded into the request function.
Billing	• One of the key differentiators to cloud computing is reinvigorating the concept of utility computing, which in essence equates to "pay only for what you use."
	• In the service delivery phase, there will be design elements to tie the service portal to the billing mechanism.
	• Security design has to be conducted to ensure that the touch points between the service portal and the billing systems are secure.

Source: Open Web Application Security Project, "The OWASP Top Ten Project," accessed June 28, 2012, https://www.owasp.org/index.php/Category:OW ASP_Top_Ten_Project.

Table 5.2   Security Considerations for Secure Resource Delivery

FOCUS AREAS	SECURITY CONSIDERATIONS
Network layer	• Apply restrictive firewall rules for orchestration communication. For added security, you can run orchestration traffic on the management network as opposed to the production network. This facilitates better control and monitoring.
	• Encrypt orchestration network traffic where possible. Orchestration data packets have critical information such as credentials and administrative access commands that can cause significant impact in the wrong hands.
Hypervisor layer	• Communicate orchestration commands on dedicated and controlled interfaces.
	• Ensure secure communication between orchestration engine and hypervisor management. Validate communication handshake and authentication protocol (depending on the orchestration engine).
	• Establish fault, error, and integrity checks for orchestration request prior to provisioning.
	• Isolate automated virtual zones in accordance with security requirements.
Storage layer	• Secure communication between orchestration engine and storage area network (SAN) management. Validate communication handshake and authentication protocol (depending on the orchestration engine).
	• Establish fault, error, and integrity checks for orchestration request prior to provisioning.
	• Isolate automated LUNs in accordance with security requirements.

5.3.3 Secure Orchestration Management

The orchestration management console is where the various automation workflows are created, managed, and operationalized. If compromised, the state of your production environments could be significantly disrupted. It is imperative that the management console be effectively secured.

Focus on the areas shown in Table 5.3 when securing the orchestration management console.

5.3.4 Security Monitoring

A multipronged approach to monitoring must be implemented to ensure the integrity of orchestration activities. As noted, orchestration brings together the various layers of network, hypervisor, operating systems, storage, and potentially applications. In each of these layers, the monitoring activities shown in Table 5.4 should be deployed.

Table 5.3 Security Considerations for Secure Orchestration Management

FOCUS AREAS	SECURITY CONSIDERATIONS
Network environment	• Firewall rules should be highly restrictive to isolate the orchestration management console to a management network and only allow access to appropriate administrators. • Establish multifactor authentication to access the management network. This can be accomplished using a VPN gateway and using two-factor authentication prior to allowing network access.
OS layer	• Harden the OS that runs the orchestration management software. Only turn on required services. Adjust default settings. Regularly patch the OS. • Install host-based intrusion detection on the system layer to monitor system level intrusions. • Enable detailed logging to track system activities and off-load the logs to a centralized log or Security Information Event Manager (SIEM) to avoid tampering by cloud administrators. • Conduct periodic user review for system layer administrative access.
Application security	• Enforce multifactor authentication for access to cloud orchestration console. The console may be accessed over a web presentation layer and by logging on to the host. Protect both layers of access with the VPN gateway. • Enforce role-based access control for different roles within the cloud orchestration console (more about this in the next section). • Enable detailed logging to track orchestration administrative activities and off-load the logs to a centralized log or SIEM to avoid tampering by cloud administrators.

Table 5.4   Security Considerations for Secure Monitoring

FOCUS AREAS	SECURITY CONSIDERATIONS
Access monitoring	• Each layer of the orchestration infrastructure has a user account component.
	• The self-service cloud portal where users log on to request their IT services must have user monitoring enabled. It is important not only to detect anomalous activities at the request layer, but also to ensure that disputes around billing and approvals can be resolved.
	• The cloud orchestration software runs on OS, which has either local or domain accounts. These accounts have to be validated and monitored on a regular basis for appropriate use. Compromise to privileged accounts or rogue administrators at the system layer can be a significant security breach for the orchestration components.
	• The cloud orchestration management interface has different user roles to design workflows, manage orchestration activities, troubleshoot issues, etc. User activities conducted within the cloud orchestration tool must be monitored to ensure the integrity of the orchestration process.
	• The network devices within the private cloud environment are accessed via user accounts that need to be monitored. Pay special attention to firewall management access.
	• The SAN and hypervisor management consoles must also be monitored for rogue access.
	• At the minimum, monitor failed logons. Successful logons are also important to keep for the purposes of time-stamping administrative activities and successful break-in attempts. If possible, log administrative tasks in the orchestration management console.
Threat monitoring	• Intrusion detection systems (IDSs) should be deployed at the network level for your private cloud environment to detect threats.
	• We recommend deploying host-based intrusion detection at the self-service portal, orchestration management, and hypervisor management servers to have added host level protection.
	• Turn on application level logging and monitoring from the various management consoles (orchestration, hypervisor, SAN, network).
	• Aggregate activity data from firewalls, IDS (network and hosts), and application logs from management to consoles to the SIEM for correlation. Also send all access monitoring data to the SIEM for correlation.
	• Activate both signature detection and anomalous monitoring and assign the right levels of alerting and triage.
Fault monitoring	• Orchestration is a complex process that requires every step of the highly coordinated workflow to be successful in order for the auto-provisioning to occur.

(continued)

Table 5.4   Security Considerations for Secure Monitoring (continued)

FOCUS AREAS	SECURITY CONSIDERATIONS
Fault monitoring	• The steps in a workflow must be configured to be fault tolerant and have graceful ways of failing, notifying, and recovering from the failure (either manual or automated). • Since a major tenet of security is the availability of the system, fault monitoring is a key to detect any failures in the stepwise orchestration workflow process to ensure the detection and recovery of failures.

6

ENCRYPTION SERVICES

6.1 Holistic Encryption Strategy

Encryption is driven by compliance requirements and data threats. Senate Bill 1386, which became effective on July 1, 2003, mandated that notification must be made to California residents if there is reasonable cause to suspect the breach of their unencrypted personal information. The operative word is *unencrypted*. Many companies have moved to encrypt personal information to avoid the hefty costs and reputational damage of breach notification. The Health Information Technology for Economic and Clinical Health Act (HITECH) enacted in 2009 to complement the Health Insurance Portability and Accountability Act (HIPAA) has encryption implications. Similar to SB1386, HITECH requires breach notification for unencrypted data of electronic health information. Noncompliance can lead to civil penalties that can extend to $250,000 per violation and up to $1.5 million for repeated offenses. The Payment Card Industry Data Security Standard (PCI-DSS) also has specific encryption requirements for securing credit card data during transport, in storage, and in backup tapes. Noncompliance leads to fines and potential business impact. The Ponemon Institute's 2011 data breach report[1] estimated the organizational cost of a data breach at $5.4 million, with a per record cost of $194. This per record cost varies from industry to industry (Figure 6.1).

Depending on your industry silo, you may need to take encryption more seriously than others due to the cost of notification.

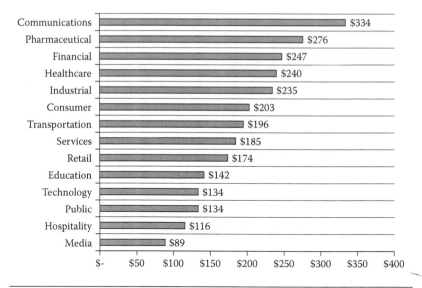

Figure 6.1   Per capita cost by industry classification of benchmarked companies. (From the Ponemon Institute LLC, "2011 Cost of Data Breach Study United States," accessed June 28, 2012, http://bit.ly/xBF6vr.)

When planning your private cloud deployment, be sure to incorporate a holistic encryption strategy that covers:

- Reducing the scope of encryption: The first step to a good encryption strategy is not to encrypt at all.
- Transport layer encryption: Identify points in your private cloud communication that need to be encrypted.
- Data layer encryption: Have a holistic strategy to encrypt structured and unstructured data.
- Key management life cycle: Establish an end-to-end process for managing and protecting encryption keys.

6.2 Scope Reduction

Before encrypting the data, ask the business or application owner whether it is necessary for that data to be there. If the data cannot be eliminated, probe to see if that data can be truncated or tokenized. Many times, the business does not require the entire length of that confidential data to be there. This is especially true in the case of credit card numbers and social security numbers. Credit card numbers are used at the point of transaction and stored for account management purposes. These numbers could be hashed or truncated to the first or last four numbers, rendering them useless to data thieves. Assign a security engineer or architect to the private cloud project to have him or her vet the necessity of having confidential data types in scope. The goal of this exercise is to reduce the footprint of data to protect, thus minimizing the attack surface or tacking on the financial, performance, and administrative costs of encryption.

6.3 Transport Layer Encryption

Transport layer encryption is about data on the move. The five major manifestations of encrypting data on the move are:

- Secure Socket Layer (SSL)
- Virtual private networks (VPNs)
- Secure shell (SSH)
- Secure File Transfer Protocol (SFTP)
- Transport Layer Security (TLS)

6.3.1 Secure Socket Layer (SSL)

This has been a standard operating procedure for years, so we will not expound on this in great length, except these four points:

- Implement SSL whenever there's confidential traffic over web servers or unsecured lines.
- Have a systematic way of handling expiration and reissuance of SSL certificates so you don't disrupt the business.
- Implement SSL for administrative console web traffic.
- Be sure to use industry-accepted SSL standards. When unsure, refer to latest updates of the National Institute of Standards and Technology (NIST). The current guidance in NIST SP800-52[2] recommends SSL v3 or TLS 1.0.

6.3.2 Virtual Private Networks (VPNs)

In the context of private cloud, VPN could be used to provide the following capabilities:

- Site-to-site connection: This capability secures two points of communication. In a private cloud implementation, you may have to allow business partner connections to transfer data or offer shared services.

- End user remote access: Your end users might want to access your private cloud capability from outside of your network. Use an SSL VPN or IPsec client to secure the communication back into your network. Enforce posture checking on the SSL VPN connection so that you can validate the client at the source. If it is a known client, you may allow more access. If it is an unknown client (such as a kiosk in an airport or coffee shop), provide a more restrictive access to limit your liability.

- Administrator VPN: A VPN gateway can be established to provide a choke point for all administrative access within the private cloud. This choke point could also be used to enforce multifactor authentication and ensure that administrators of IT are carefully screened and audited prior to managing your cloud infrastructure.

6.3.3 Secure Shell (SSH)

SSH is commonly used by administrators for remote console access. It may seem that VPN and SSH are redundant. However, if telnet is permitted instead of SSH, intracloud traffic will be unencrypted. A telnet session containing administrator credentials can be sniffed in clear text. Getting rid of telnet all together and enforcing SSH as a minimum standard is necessary even with the overlay of VPN.

6.3.4 Secure File Transfer Protocol (SFTP)

If there are requirements to securely transfer files to and from your private cloud, ensure that you establish an SFTP process:

- Establish a user management process to clearly identify and control user access.

- Establish onboarding, de-provisioning, and user certification processes.
- Establish appropriate access permissions and folder isolation for SFTP users.
- Enforce data cleanup of SFTP folders on a periodic basis.

6.3.5 *Transport Layer Security (TLS)*

TLS encryption is typically used to encrypt SMTP traffic over two e-mail gateways. This might not be specific to your private cloud implementation, but it is covered here to be comprehensive.

6.4 Data Layer Encryption

Encrypting the transport layer gets the data from point A to point B safely. Data layer encryption is about protecting the data when they are at rest. In a private cloud scenario, your tenants are most likely the various business units within your enterprise. Some of you may have requirements to house different business partners or corporate customers within your cloud. These requirements point to the need to create a secure multitenant environment, one of the key characteristics of cloud architecture. Your constituents expect their data to be protected from other tenants due to the varying levels of compliance required by different tenants. Segmentation provides a level of separation, but encryption of the data offers layered protection to maintain confidentiality within a multitenant environment.

The following categories of data encryption methods are available for your private cloud implementation:

- Database encryption
- File encryption
- Network-attached encryption
- Disk encryption
- Virtualization encryption

Your approach to encryption has to align to your compliance requirements, existing architecture, pain points, budgets, and other constraints. To that end, different encryption solutions might work better for you than others. The following subsections describe the types of data encryption technology available to you, along with the factors that may influence your decision, depending on your needs.

6.4.1 Database Encryption

Major database vendors such as Oracle and Microsoft SQL have built-in encryption capabilities within their applications. The prominent database encryption methodology is called Transparent Data Encryption (TDE). TDE provides database management systems with the ability to encrypt the entire database, or to only encrypt certain columns. Factor in the considerations shown in Table 6.1 when choosing table space encryption (encrypting the entire database) versus column space encryption.

Our recommendation is to choose table space encryption unless you have a very specific reason to use column space encryption. The performance, simplicity, and flexibility of using table space encryption outweigh most benefits offered by encrypting specific columns. Some auditors might argue that table space encryption is insufficient for protecting against database administrator access to data. Our advice is to clarify the requirements with the auditor and delineate the differences between encryption and database access control. Encryption provides protection for data at rest. Access management provides protection by only allowing the right individuals or applications to use the data. Access management is better served by deploying a database access management toolset, along with a strong access monitoring component.

6.4.2 File Encryption

While TDE works for structured data in databases, you may have a business need to provide encryption for unstructured data. Most operating systems provide file level encryption as a native function. This works at a per user level, but may not be suitable as an enterprise solution. Furthermore, the grade of native encryption capabilities is typically not good enough to meet regulatory and industry standards.

Often times, files that contain confidential or nonpublic personal information (NPPI) are stored in unstructured data formats such as

Table 6.1   Table Space versus Column Space Encryption

AREAS	TABLE SPACE ENCRYPTION	COLUMN/CELL SPACE ENCRYPTION
Index	• Has the ability to encrypt any index type. • Does not interfere with application indexing function.	• Can only encrypt specific index types. • Additionally, encrypted columns cannot be used as index keys for the application. • Validate with the specifications outlined by your database management system.
Data type	• No restrictions on data types. • The entire table space is encrypted.	• Only applies to specific data types and data length. • Validate with the specifications outlined by your database management system.
Performance	• With table space encryption, the entire table is encrypted. With column space encryption, you select applicable fields. • The two major database vendors quote a performance impact of between 3% and 5%. • Oracle 11 supports leveraging native hardware crypto acceleration to increase performance when used with specific Intel® platforms.	• Depending on how much of the data are being encrypted, the performance impact varies. • Performance is more noticeable due to the on-demand nature of column level encryption. • Performance degradation is dependent on the application logic, data access, data type, and workload specifics. • Our recommendation is to do thorough performance testing with the specific application in question.
Security	• Compromise of a single key could unlock the entire database. • Automatic decryption does not provide data-specific protection. With that said, access control is not to be confused with encryption. Encryption provides protection when data are at rest.	• Data not decrypted until used. • Explicit key management to allow specific users or application to see specific data types.
Storage size	• Minimal impact to storage size. • High-compression ratio because data are decrypted when compressed.	• Potential storage impact of 1 to 52 bytes per encrypted value. • Low-compression ratio because data stay encrypted when being compressed.

(continued)

Table 6.1   Table Space versus Column Space Encryption (continued)

AREAS	TABLE SPACE ENCRYPTION	COLUMN/CELL SPACE ENCRYPTION
Configuration and administration	• Configuration and setup are done at the onset. • Ongoing administration is minimal. • Periodic key rotation activities.	• Administrative overhead of managing different keys per different columns. • New columns that need to be encrypted require configuration setup. • Potential user and passphrase reset management. • Key rotation is more complex due to impact on actively used databases.
Query optimization	• Does not interfere with query optimization or range scans.	• Cannot accommodate query optimization and range scans.
Hardware security module (HSM)	• Options to store on the database server or use a hardware security module (HSM).	• Oracle does not support HSM for column space encryption. • Microsoft SQL 2008 supports external key management for both cell space and table space encryption using its enterprise key management (EKM) module.

Word or Excel documents. If you do not provide an enterprise solution to secure and host these files, they will proliferate all over your environment, exposing you to the risk of data breaches. When building an enterprise solution for file encryption, consider:

- Centralized management: Using the native encryption, you leave the encryption management to the end users. You need to effectively manage users and encrypted files, folders, and volumes from a single pane of glass.
- Integration with a hardware security module (HSM): There are a number of stand-alone solutions out there, but consider a single key management system for all your encryption needs and invest in a robust HSM to manage, protect, and rotate your keys.
- Ease of use: Consider encryption requirements that provide transparent security where the users are not aware that they are being protected. There are solutions that work seamlessly to use pass-through credentials for decryption and integrate with your user repository to check for authentication or group

membership. This reduces administrative overhead for user provisioning as well as password support.

- Multiplatform support: Be sure to validate that the encryption capabilities can work seamlessly on all the various OSs you support in your environment.
- Workflows: Develop the appropriate workflows to facilitate user requests, administrative functions, and key management.

6.4.3 Encryption Appliances

Encryption appliances provide a way for cryptographic functions to be performed on the network. The application logic makes a programmatic call to the encryption module on the appliance to encrypt data prior to storing it in the database. Here are some of the key factors to consider when using an encryption appliance:

- Performance: Network-attached encryption devices are specialized appliances built for the purpose of performing cryptographic functions. Some of these devices can encrypt at near wire speeds. Additionally, the off-loading of cryptographic functions to an appliance means that your servers are not taking the performance hit from encryption functions.
- Centralized: The encryption appliance can be used by different tenants on your private cloud. You still need to provide the appropriate segregation of environments and access, but you do not need disparate solutions in different areas of your environment. Consider solutions that can synchronize management for devices deployed across various locations around the world. For performance reasons, you may need to deploy these devices closer to their user base.
- Integration to HSMs: Most of these encryption devices integrate with HSMs for key management. Some of them even act as an HSM for your environment. Depending on the size of your deployment, scale this solution accordingly.
- Impact to applications: These solutions provide several ways to call the encryption function. At the web layer, it could be a programmatic call that sends out a field to be encrypted prior to storing it into the database. For file servers, it could be

acting through an agent. Basically, the centralized encryption appliance will affect your code and your endpoints. Consider the impact as well as your exit strategy.

- Licensing costs: These appliances may be licensed per connector, per cryptographic functions, or a one-time appliance fee with maintenance. Match your current and future requirements to the licensing model to ensure that you do not incur huge licensing penalties.
- High availability: You need to have a highly robust and dependable solution in order to put these encryption devices in the middle of your application and database layers. Build a fault-tolerant system to accommodate hardware, software, and connectivity issues. Ensure that the code at the application layer is able to handle exceptions as well.

Some of these encryption appliances are being deployed as VM appliances. Vet out the performance and input/output implications, but seriously consider going with the VM appliance in a cloud environment. The VM equivalent will be able to capitalize on the agility, performance, and high availability of virtualized computing.

6.4.4 Disk Encryption

Disk encryption is a hardware function of encrypting the entire disk instead of encrypting files, volumes, or table spaces. This is analogous to hard-disk encryption deployed at the laptop level; however, for the purposes of cloud, we are transposing its capability to storage area network (SAN) and network-attached storage (NAS). Deployments vary depending on the vendor. Some vendors, like EMC, integrate the solution as an additional module within the storage management solution (Figure 6.2).

Other vendors, like Brocade, deploy a SAN encryption switch to encrypt data at near wire speed on the SAN fabric between the host (or VM) and the logical unit numbers (LUNs) (Figure 6.3). Data are encrypted on the switch prior to being stored in the SAN.

If your goal for encryption is to comply with regulatory or industry standards, make sure you engage your auditors or third-party security assessors before embarking on the path of disk or

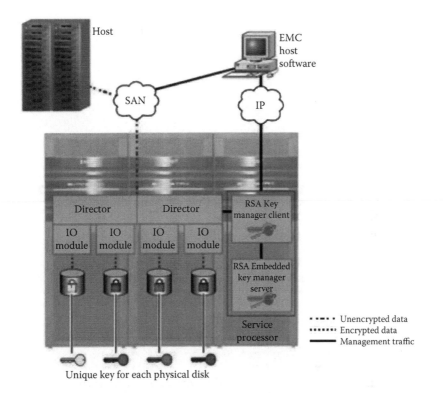

Figure 6.2 EMC symmetric encryption architecture. (From EMC Corporation, "EMC Symmetrix Data at Rest Encryption Achieves FIPS 140-2 Validation," accessed June 28, 2012, http://www.storagenewsletter.com/news/systems/emc-symmetrix-encryption-flips-140-2.)

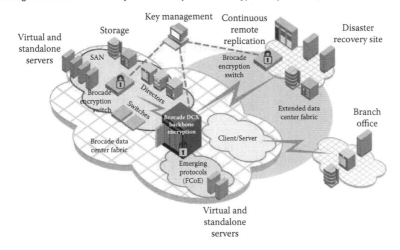

Figure 6.3 Brocade encryption switch. (From Brocade, "Broacade Encryption Switch," accessed June 28, 2012, http://www.brocade.com/products/all/switches/product-details/encryption-switch/index.page.)

SAN encryption. The requirements often cover the entire scope of the encryption life cycle, including proper key management. Go through each requirement line by line with your disk encryption vendors. Ask your vendors whether they have a white paper outlining their compliance to regulatory or industry guidance such as PCI-DSS. Disk encryption in particular is called out by PCI in requirement 3.4.1, which states, "If disk encryption is used (rather than file- or column-level database encryption), logical access must be managed independently of native operating-system access-control mechanisms (for example, by not using local-user account databases). Decryption keys must not be tied to user accounts."[3] There are a number of other encryption and key management specific requirements that have to be adhered to. It is imperative that you validate this not only with your vendor, but also with your PCI qualified security assessor (QSA).

6.4.5 *Virtualization Encryption*

The agent-based implementation is similar to preboot disk encryption. Basically, the agent is loaded inside the virtual machine and intercepts the boot-up sequence of the virtual instance. The agent then runs a preboot authentication sequence to validate and apply the appropriate encryption domain for that virtual instance. Essentially, the encryption domain can act as a segmentation mechanism on your private cloud for your compliance-heavy business units or environments. By wrapping an encryption domain around these systems, you can meet the requirement of encrypting the data for the entire stack. As with the other encryption technologies, just encrypting the data alone is not sufficient to meet most compliance requirements. Ensure that the vendor can meet the entire encryption and key management requirements. If unsure, validate with your auditor or qualified security assessor.

Consider the following factors when reviewing agent-based virtual instance encryption:

- Vet the key management mechanisms for the encryption solution.

- Ensure that keys are being distributed securely during runtime.
- Ensure that encryption keys are protected when stored.
- Validate access control for key usage.
- Ensure the auditability and traceability of key usage.
- Understand the key rotation, backup, and recovery functions.
- Find out if the solution can integrate with an HSM so that key management is centralized across your enterprise.
- Understand the impact to your VM environment.
  - Validate that the agent can run on your choice of hypervisor and OS flavors.
  - Understand the performance impact of the encryption. Some vendors have quoted around 5 to 10% impact.
  - Validate how the encryption will affect your VM functions. For example, can the de-duplication function be performed if the virtual instance is encrypted? Does encryption break the VM snapshot function? Ask your vendor to list the hypervisor functions that will be impacted by their encryption product.
- Plan for the impact to your business environment.
  - Clarify the operational impact of the various encryption infrastructure components failing. What happens if the preboot authentication fails? What happens if the agents do not load? What happens if the agent cannot reach the management console?
  - Develop a highly available and fault-tolerant design.
  - Establish production monitoring to proactively alert when key components fail.
  - Securely back up your key infrastructure.

Some vendors have the ability to extend the encryption modules to both private and public clouds. The agent-based aspect of this solution facilitates an easier deployment because there is minimal dependency on the public cloud's back end. Key management can be retained within the enterprise with a key distribution appliance that sits in the public cloud.

6.5 Key Management Life Cycle

In recent years, PCI-DSS requirements 3.4 to 3.6 have been the major force driving the companies toward secure cryptographic key management. These requirements have shaped encryption vendors as well as how IT organizations implement their key management technology and processes.

Let's examine the PCI requirements (see Table 6.2) and take a look at how each requirement could influence your design and deployment decisions.

Another reference for key management requirements can be found in the NIST Special Publication 800-57[4] entitled "Recommendation for Key Management" (comes in Part 1 and Part 2). NIST SP 800-57 provides a comprehensive guide for designing your private cloud, key management infrastructure.

According to NIST SP 800-57, there are four main phases to a key's life cycle (Figure 6.4):

1. Preoperational phase: Keys are not in production. Key attributes are compiled to associate a particular key to its owner or function.
2. Operational phase: Key has been generated and is in use.
3. Postoperational phase: Keys are no longer in production but are kept around for special circumstances (typically data recovery). Keys in this phase are typically archived when not processing data.
4. Destroyed phase: Keys are no longer needed because the data protected by the key are destroyed or the keys have been compromised. The key will be deleted; however, attributes about the key (key name, type, usage period, etc.) may be retained for historical knowledge.

Table 6.2 PCI Requirements for Key Management

PCI REQUIREMENT	IMPLICATION
3.4.1 If disk encryption is used (rather than file or column level database encryption), logical access must be managed independently of native operating system access control mechanisms (for example, by not using local user account databases). Decryption keys must not be tied to user accounts.	• Back to the topic of disk encryption, this PCI requirement allows the use of disk encryption, but explicitly calls for separation of key access from the native OS. • The best solution for this is to choose a disk encryption vendor that can off-load key storage and management to an external hardware security module (HSM).
3.5 Protect encryption keys used for encryption of cardholder data against both disclosure and misuse.	• Designate and train your key custodians to safeguard the keys.
3.5.1 Restrict access to cryptographic keys to the fewest number of custodians necessary.	• Ensure that clear roles and responsibilities are defined for your key custodians.
3.5.2 Store cryptographic keys securely in the fewest possible locations and forms.	• Use an HSM to protect encryption keys, restrict access, and centralize key storage.
3.6 Fully document and implement all key management processes and procedures for cryptographic keys used for encryption of cardholder data, including the following:	• Develop standard operating procedure (SOP) documentation for your key management functions.
3.6.1 Generation of strong cryptographic keys. 3.6.2 Secure cryptographic key distribution. 3.6.3 Secure cryptographic key storage. 3.6.4 Cryptographic key changes for keys that have reached the end of their crypto period, as defined by the associated application vendor or key owner, and based on industry best practices and guidelines (for example, NIST Special Publication 800-57). 3.6.5 Retirement or replacement (for example, archiving, destruction, or revocation) of keys as deemed necessary when the integrity of the key has been weakened (for example, departure of an employee with knowledge of a clear-text key), or keys are suspected of being compromised.	• Ensure that the SOP covers all the relevant topics for the four phases of the cryptographic key life cycle: preoperational phase, operational phase, postoperational phase, and destroyed phase (more about this later). • Most of these key management functions can be relegated to a good HSM. It is important to note that not all HSMs are created equal. • Select a vendor that can automate key rotation without impacting production. • Select a vendor that has strong role-based access control for key management access. Additionally, the vendor should also have dual control and split knowledge capabilities to operate master key functions. • Select a vendor that has tamper-evident storage. This is critical for a sound audit trail of key generation, usage, rotation, archiving, and destruction operations.

(continued)

Table 6.2   PCI Requirements for Key Management (continued)

PCI REQUIREMENT	IMPLICATION
3.6.6 If manual clear-text cryptographic key management operations are used, these operations must be managed using split knowledge and dual control (for example, requiring two or three people, each knowing only their own key component, to reconstruct the whole key).	• Select a vendor that can integrate to your ticketing and monitoring capabilities.
3.6.7 Prevention of unauthorized substitution of cryptographic keys.	• Have formal sign-off for roles and responsibilities around critical key administration.
3.6.8 Requirement for cryptographic key custodians to formally acknowledge that they understand and accept their key custodian responsibilities.	

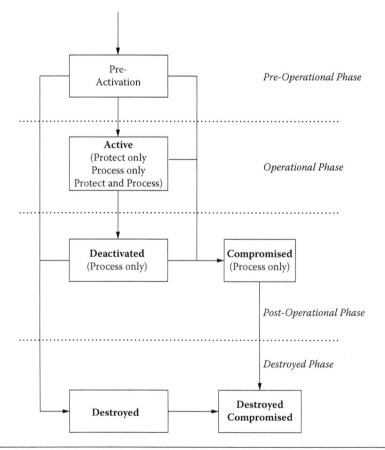

Figure 6.4   NIST SP 800-57 key management phases.

References

1. Ponemon Institute LLC. 2011 cost of data breach study United States. Accessed June 28, 2012, http://bit.ly/xBF6vr.
2. C. Michael Chernick, Charles Edington III, Matthew J. Fanto, and Rob Rosenthal. Guidelines for the selection and use of transport layer security (TLS) implementations. Accessed June 28, 2012, http://csrc.nist.gov/publications/nistpubs/800-52/SP800-52.pdf.
3. PCI Standards Council. Understanding the intent of the requirements. Accessed June 28, 2012, https://www.pcisecuritystandards.org/documents/navigating_dss_v20.pdf.
4. Elaine Barker, William Barker, William Burr, William Polk, and Miles Smid. Recommendation for key management part 1: General. Accessed June 28, 2012, http://csrc.nist.gov/publications/PubsDrafts.html#SP-800-57-Part%201.

7

THREAT INTELLIGENCE

7.1 Security Threats to Private Cloud

As noted earlier, we have threat actors that have both the motives and the means to attack your private cloud environment. Cyber criminals are focused on finding valuable data assets that they can monetize. Hacktivists are looking to disrupt and embarrass your organization. Hired hands are specifically targeting your environment to achieve any objective that they are being paid for.

These threat actors seek out vulnerabilities in your private cloud implementation and seek to exploit them. There are disruptive attacks and payload-driven attacks. Disruptive attacks, typically launched by hacktivists, are designed to cause downtime and draw attention. The most prominent disruptive attack is distributed denial of service attacks. The more common form of attack that is used by hacktivists, hackers, and cyber criminals is payload-driven attacks. These attacks go after payloads such as data assets, intellectual property, e-mail communication, etc. The typical phases in a payload-driven attack are as follows:

- Reconnaissance: This is the information gathering stage of an attack.
- Infiltration: The attacker finds a foothold in your environment.
- Expansion: The attacker seeks to go deeper into your environment to gain more footing and to look for a payload (typically information assets). He or she is also covering his or her tracks to avoid detection.
- Exfiltration: The attacker orchestrates the extraction of stolen goods.

Table 7.1 captures a sample of the threats that may impact your private cloud implementation in each one of the attack phases.

Table 7.1   Attack Phases and Associated Threats

ATTACK PHASE	THREATS
Reconnaissance	• Conduct scans against your network to reveal possible open ports to exploit.
	• Conduct scans against your Internet-facing servers to fingerprint your web, e-mail, and remote access servers.
	• More targeted attacks will collect information about your executives and administrators.
	• Collect information from public registrars. Knowing who registered the domain names for your company gives the attacker a specific target.
	• Social engineering on your support or helpdesk departments.
	• Scoping your data center or business offices to gain physical access.
	• Reading blog postings by your employees, especially your IT administrators.
	• Leveraging insiders, outsourcers, or partners to gain more domain knowledge.
Infiltration	• Phishing or malware attacks against your end users to gain entry into your enterprise network.
	• Spear phishing or malware attacks against your administrators or executives to gain credentials or useful information assets.
	• Exploit web, e-mail, or remote access server vulnerabilities to gain remote control.
	• Exploit application and database logic to gain access to data assets.
	• Gain access via a partner network that has weaker security.
Expansion	• Malware will try to contact the bot controller to indicate access, upload intelligence, and download tools to expand footprint and cover tracks.
	• Some malware has demonstrated VM fingerprinting capabilities to identify the virtualization technology it is running on.
	• Download scanners or use native OS tools to survey network and server assets.
	• Expand malware to other servers.
	• Find and exploit payload.
	• Find and exploit administrative credentials.
Exfiltration	• Systematically send data back to controller without being detected.
	• Search through file servers for valuable data.
	• Compromise e-mail server(s) to access e-mails.

Exposure can also take place due to unintentional or human factors, such as:

- Losing laptop or mobile devices or leaving them unattended
- Losing unencrypted backup tapes
- Losing confidential documents (paper)
- Choosing easy-to-guess passwords

- Moving confidential material outside corporate systems (not for malicious intent)
- Allowing people to shoulder browse

To effectively manage threats in your private cloud, you need to rely on layered protection. The two-pronged attack is to prevent breaches and improve early detection of threats.

7.2 Threat Prevention Strategies

Your private cloud implementation is no different than your traditional data center protection. Focus on creating defense in depth, instill sound processes, and raise security awareness across the enterprise (Table 7.2).

Complete prevention is not actually the panacea. You may not have the budget and staffing to deploy all the aforementioned toolsets for prevention. You may also encounter resistance from your business units for trying to place more security tools, which may cut into their usability, performance, flexibility, and time to market. Furthermore, preventative tools have been known to cause production outages. You need to work within the parameters of your own budget to prioritize your risks accordingly and spend money where you get the biggest bang for the buck. Also, this subsection called out preventative measures that provide a proactive posture against threats. Eventually, attackers will find ways around your defenses. We will now take a look at capabilities to detect threats before they become breaches.

7.3 Threat Detection Toolset

A typical data breach attack is multiphased and happens over time typically. In each one of the attack phases, you can deploy tools to detect, correlate, and alert of malicious activities. Let's examine the toolset corresponding to each attack phase (Table 7.3).

Having a range of tools to detect an attack may be a disservice because you now have to parse through copious amounts of logs and alerts to find an actual threat. Data are meaningless unless they are intelligent.

Table 7.2 Preventative Measures

ATTACK TYPES	PREVENTATIVE MEASURES
Conduct scans against your network to reveal possible open ports to exploit.	• Configure your Internet-facing firewalls to block or limit visibility into your corporate network. • Ensure that your orchestration policies adequately segment demilitarized zone (DMZ) environments from the rest of production. Create a validation point in the workflow for the provisioning of Internet-facing virtual networks. • Install an intrusion prevention system to automatically block common threats. • You can also hide your entire web-facing presence behind a content delivery network. These service providers will act as a proxy for all incoming traffic.
Targeted attacks against executives and administrators. Collect information from public registrars. Social engineering on your support or helpdesk departments. Reading blog postings by your employees, especially your IT administrators. Phishing attacks against your end users.	• Develop a dedicated security awareness program for high-value targets in your enterprise: • Executives and their assistants • System, network, and application administrators • Call centers and support desks • Human resource and payroll departments • Developers of intellectual property • Create a security culture in your organization by being innovative with the continuous learning and awareness (as opposed to the annual, compulsory computer-based training).
Malware attacks against your end users to gain entry into your enterprise network.	• Focus on building a robust endpoint for laptops. • Enforce strong passwords or multifactor authentication to access endpoints. • Do not grant local administrative rights. • Regularly perform system updates and antivirus patches. • Have encryption for data at rest. • Have host-based intrusion prevention. • Use data leakage protection (e.g., copying to USB). • Enforce mobile security for smart phones and tablets.

(continued)

Table 7.2 Preventative Measures (continued)

ATTACK TYPES	PREVENTATIVE MEASURES
	• Invest in malware inspection technologies that examine web content for malware prior to allowing users to connect to it.
	• Implement web content filtering in the cloud to prevent end users from browsing malicious sites when they are not protected behind the corporate network.
Conduct scans against your Internet-facing servers to fingerprint your web, e-mail, and remote access servers.	• Ensure that production systems are hardened and patched within your virtual machine templates.
Exploit web, e-mail, or remote access server vulnerabilities to gain remote control.	• As part of the orchestration workflows, ensure that a security review is conducted prior to allowing users to deploy Internet-facing servers.
	• Ensure that your physical and virtual appliances are patched.
	• Perform periodic security vulnerability assessments or penetration tests from the Internet to validate your defenses.
	• Implement web access firewalls to prevent layer 7 attacks.
	• Perform web application testing from the Internet.
	• Institute sound user access management for production access covering applications, systems, and networks. User management includes:
	• Provisioning
	• Periodic access certification to validate that the access is current and that the roles are appropriate
	• Transfers and terminations
	• Inactivity and deletion of accounts
	• Processes for partner, contractor, and temporary access
Exploit application and database logic to gain access to data assets.	• Implement orchestration policies that deploy firewalls to effectively segment your network to prevent easy traversal of your cloud environment.
Search through file servers for valuable data.	• Build a secure software development life cycle program within your enterprise.

(continued)

Table 7.2 Preventative Measures (continued)

ATTACK TYPES	PREVENTATIVE MEASURES
Compromise exchange server to access e-mails.	• Incorporate a code scanning tool to locate code vulnerabilities (and instruct developers to correct them) prior to production.
Download scanners or use native OS tools to survey network and server assets.	• Ensure that applications and databases are patched regularly.
Expand malware to other servers.	• Conduct internal vulnerability assessment testing.
Find and exploit payload.	• Encrypt relevant data in the database and file servers.
Gain access via a partner network that has weaker security.	• Institute contracts to ensure that your third parties and downstream providers abide by your security standards.
	• Firewall your environment from your partner networks and only allow explicit access.
	• If your cloud is allowing the use of application programming interfaces (APIs) or web services to interact with your applications, look into deploying Extensible Markup Language (XML) firewalls to thwart attacks against exposed web services.
	• Install an intrusion prevention system.
Some malware have demonstrated VM fingerprinting capabilities to identify the virtualization technology of the infected host.	• Segment your internal network to prevent easy access to sensitive areas.
	• Implement VM hardening guidelines to ensure that both your virtual hosts and guests are properly secured.
Find and exploit administrative credentials.	
	• Place your VM administration on a separate management network that requires multifactor authentication to access.
	• Encrypt all administrative traffic. Use virtual private network (VPN), Secure Socket Layer (SSL), or secure shell (SSH) for administrative activities.
Systematically send data back to the controller without being detected.	• Configure a firewall or Internet proxy to only allow outbound connections that have been explicitly permitted.
	• Implement a web content filtering appliance to inspect all outgoing traffic connections (including SSL).
	• Implement data leakage prevention (DLP) to block sensitive data from leaving your environment. Deploy DLP at your egress points, e-mail environment, and endpoints.

(continued)

Table 7.2 Preventative Measures (continued)

ATTACK TYPES	PREVENTATIVE MEASURES
DDoS attack on your environment.	• You can place your Internet-facing server behind a content delivery provider that offers DDoS protection. They have significantly more bandwidth and an arrangement upstream with ISPs to divert, block, or absorb most DDoS attacks. • Or you can procure specialized DDoS protection appliances that have the heuristics to separate DDoS traffic from regular traffic and allow your production environment to continue operating while blocking or thwarting the DDoS attack.

7.4 Making Threat Detection Intelligent

The anatomy of an attack reveals that if you detect the intrusion earlier in its life cycle, you can usually stop the hacking activity before it causes any real damage. The goal here is not just to collect volumes of security data. It is not even to parse those data and make them meaningful. The goal is to get to actionable intelligence where once you have meaningful security data, you can immediately mobilize threat analysts and the Computer Security Incident Response Team (CSIRT) to take proactive action to contain and eradicate the threat. To do this, you need to incorporate the following components into your threat intelligence system (Figure 7.1):

• Security Information Event Manager (SIEM): Centralize your log storage and heuristics for indexing, filtering, and funneling security data into actionable intelligence. A good SIEM deployment is at the heart of an effective threat intelligence system.
• Infrastructure logs: These logs do not necessarily provide security-specific data but contextual data from your firewalls, network switches, virtual clusters, operating systems, identity repositories, etc.
• Security toolset data: These logs are from your security-specific devices. They are often prefiltered and have decent accuracy associated with the event. Correlating security data

Table 7.3   Detective Measures

ATTACK PHASE	THREAT DETECTION TOOLS
Reconnaissance	• Place an intrusion detection or prevention system (IDS/IPS) behind your perimeter firewalls to detect any reconnaissance activities that bypassed your first layer of defense. Explore hypervisor-based IDS/IPS to detect inter- and intra-VM network traffic. • Turn on logging of all your firewalls and send appropriate logs to a Security Information Event Manager (SIEM). Spikes in firewall CPU or connection rates could indicate a scan. • Send netflow data to your SIEM to detect anomalous patterns on your network and store historic data about source and destination addresses.
Infiltration	• Feed web application firewall (WAF) logs into your SIEM to flag potential anomalous web application behavior. Choose a WAF product that can work with database monitoring vendors to map web activities to database access. The attacker is going after your data assets, so having the ability to correlate web to database actions would increase your threat detection capabilities. If your WAF cannot do the mapping, use your SIEM correlation rules to achieve the same result. • Host-based IDS/IPS (HIDS/HIPS) is difficult to deploy due to the potential impact on production services, but it is effective in detecting threats once the attacker has managed to gain access to the host. Explore a hypervisor HIDS/HIPS that is not agent based. Hypervisor HIDS/HIPS provides detection for your virtualized platforms by detecting OS and kernel level activities without impacting your production VM servers. • Database monitoring protection can detect anomalous actions on your databases. Feed them to the SIEM to alert of unauthorized or irregular data access activities. • An alternative to HIPS/HIDS is file integrity monitoring. There are open-source solutions that identify changes to key system files that may be indicative of a rootkit, Trojan, or malware. • From an endpoint perspective, invest in malware inspection technologies that can detect infected endpoints on your enterprise as soon as they plug in to a corporate network.
Expansion	• Both your host and network IDS/IPSs are instrumental in detecting rogue scans on your network. If you are using physical network IDS/IPS, place them in your DMZ and database tiers. • Our recommendation is to invest in a hypervisor-based network and host IDS/IPS. They provide the added advantages of detecting inter- and intra-VM traffic, are dynamic, and can be embedded in your orchestration policies, and they are not disruptive to your production environment. • The key disadvantage of hypervisor-based IDS/IPSs is that they consume your hypervisor cluster resources. Set limits on their usage to avoid disruption to production systems or off-load key processing to a dedicated appliance outside the hypervisor cluster. They are also fairly new on the market, so make sure you conduct a proof of concept to vet bugs and deficiencies.

(continued)

Table 7.3 Detective Measures (continued)

ATTACK PHASE	THREAT DETECTION TOOLS
Exfiltration	• Data leakage prevention (DLP) is the best defense in detecting movement of information assets out of your network. You can set DLP to prevent or detect. Start out in detection until you have a decent level of maturity to not disrupt legitimate activities.
	• Deploy DLP at the egress points, your e-mail traffic, and your endpoints and feed into your SIEM for correlation.
	• Database monitoring tools can also detect anomalous data access behavior.

with contextual data will provide your threat analysts with a richer set of information to investigate the event.

- Assessment data: Penetration tests, vulnerability assessments, and code scanning reveal weaknesses at your network, system, and application layers. Your IT staff or developers may lag on remediating the vulnerabilities in their area. As such, being able to correlate vulnerable systems against reconnaissance or infiltration activities can help you classify the urgency of a specific event. There are free and paid services offering valuable information around the reputation of source IP addresses. Feeding these data into your SIEM can also provide you with correlated data that the source of attack is dangerous and thus must be taken seriously.

- Communication systems: Tying your SIEM to your communication systems enables you to mobilize your threat analysts or IT administrators in short order. The tie-in to your ticketing system allows for tracking and time stamping as triage is being done. Some of you have incident or case management software as well that may benefit from being able to cull data from the SIEM or the ticketing system.

- Dashboards: Portals provide instant access to your threat intelligence. You want to establish an operational portal for your security or threat analysts to be able to drill down through the SIEM for relevant and contextual data. Over time, your SIEM is going to contain valuable trend data that you want to serve up to your security or IT managers. Trend data help you to be proactive and give context to good decision making.

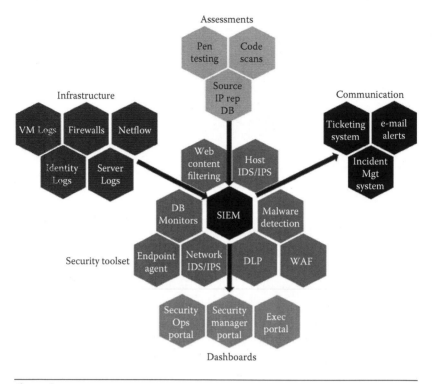

Figure 7.1   Threat intelligence model.

Last but not least, you want to establish an executive portal that provides business-relevant intelligence based on your threat data. You may also use this to hold different business units accountable for threat exposure or not keeping up with their remediation activities.

8

IDENTITY MANAGEMENT FOR PRIVATE CLOUDS

8.1 Layers of Identities

There is a vast difference between identities and accounts. An identity can be mapped to a person. An account is an arbitrary profile that has been given access to a program. A person can be mapped to many accounts depending on his or her role(s) in the organization. Nonpersons can be mapped to accounts to fulfill a programmatic function (e.g., service accounts, test accounts, etc.). Each layer within your cloud implementation has accounts that are used by identities in a designated role:

- Enterprise directory access: For most organizations, this is typically your Active Directory implementation.
- Network logons: This allows your network administrators to access network appliances. Integration with Active Directory is common here.
- Operating system (OS) local accounts: This allows users and administrators to log on locally to servers and desktops. Every guest virtual machine has local and, if joined to a domain, enterprise level accounts.
- Application level access: Every application in your cloud has local accounts from web servers to middleware to custom business applications built by your development or off-the-shelf software. Most of them can integrate into your enterprise account for authentication.
- Database accounts: This can be integrated to the enterprise directory, the local account, or a stand-alone, database access account.
- Hypervisor management accounts: This can be local to the management console or integrated with your enterprise directory.

- Virtual physical host access: Depending on the virtualization technology you choose, there is root level access to the hypervisor layer on the host servers.
- Orchestration management access: Depending on the orchestration software you choose, you may have another layer of authentication and role-based access management for logging on to the orchestration workflow interface. Most of them have integration into your enterprise directory for authentication.
- Security appliance access: Every security appliance, virtual or physical, has a local access account in addition to integration with your enterprise directory.
- Storage area network (SAN) management: Access to your SAN also requires a separate set of accounts.

Managing identities is not a trivial activity for any private cloud deployment. You need to effectively map identities to roles, and roles to appropriate entitlements across the layers of your cloud.

As if the number of accounts is not complex enough, you have myriad identities in your environment with varying levels of liability (and corresponding access governance requirements).

- Full-time and part-time employees: Require day-to-day access to do their job.
- Employees on leave of absence: Require disabling of accounts but not deletion.
- Short-term contractors: Require controlled access with expiration dates.
- Long-term contractors: Require similar access to that of an employee but must be flagged appropriately due to use of non-company equipment.
- Outsourced resources: Require specific and auditable access.
- Offshore resources: Regulatory requirements, the quality of the background checks, and the economic context of the offshoring entity are weighed when determining the level of access control for these resources.
- Outsourced onshore contractors: Require limited access that is controlled and auditable.
- Consultants: Require controlled access with expiration dates.
- Vendor engineers: May require on-site or remote access 24/7.

- Auditors: Require temporary access to validate controls.
- Business partners: Require portal or site-to-site access.
- Customers and clients: Require customer level access to their accounts on our systems.
- Affiliates: They are bound by contractual obligation but do not report to our management or human resources. Their access is limited and specific.

Effectively managing the cross-pollination of countless access types with the dizzying array of identities will require a significant portion of your resources, budget, and time. The approach to addressing the challenges of identity and access management (ID&AM) begins with a good scoping exercise.

8.2 Challenges of Disparate Identity Repositories

You private cloud initiative will naturally inherit all your identity problems of disparate user repositories across systems, applications, management nodes, security devices, and network layers. If you have done little to consolidate any of these repositories, you might want to use the private cloud project as an impetus for establishing the proper foundation for identity management. Orchestration and self-directed provisioning of computing resources will only cause the number of accounts you have in your enterprise to proliferate.

Your private cloud users and administrators probably have a number of accounts with different credentials to log on to the various systems, applications, or management consoles they need to do their jobs. Having disparate user repositories results in a number of issues:

- Inconsistent user management practices across the various cloud layers (application, systems, network, hypervisor management, SAN, etc.).
- Promotes legacy access due to the fact that each individual identity silo has to be touched for change of roles or terminations. Additionally, there is a high risk of leaving terminated users enabled. Each account has to be disabled individually as opposed to having a central place to affect change to all.
- Negative user experiences due to the number of credentials they have to memorize, change passwords to, and request for access.

- High operational costs to maintain by way of user administration, password recovery calls, toolsets to license, and the amount of duplicative effort.
- Challenges in passing user account audits due to the different way each account is being managed.
- Lack of accurate, consolidated, and meaningful information about access and identities. To map an individual to the types of access he or she has in your enterprise is a highly manual effort.
- Disparate identity repositories make automation difficult or impossible. Cloud orchestration benefits from a streamlined identity management approach.

8.3 Centralizing Identity Repositories

The goal of the central identity repository is to build a single, authoritative source to map a real person to the different types of access he or she has across your cloud environment. This real person can be an employee, a contractor, a consultant, a vendor, etc. The complexity comes in tying the various elements of identity authoritative sources to all the systems that he or she can access. To do this, a centralized identity architecture needs to be developed that can consume identity information from various identity sources, pull entitlements information from all layers of cloud components, and integrate entitlements from your cloud applications in order to effectively process the identity and entitlements data to map individual users to their varied access. Let's examine each component within the central identity repository architecture in greater detail (Figure 8.1).

8.3.1 Entitlements Aggregator

Different ID&AM solutions may have different architectures, but the concepts are transferable. The entitlements aggregator serves the following functions:

- Aggregate identity information from authoritative sources of identities.
- Aggregate entitlements information from user repositories within your cloud applications.

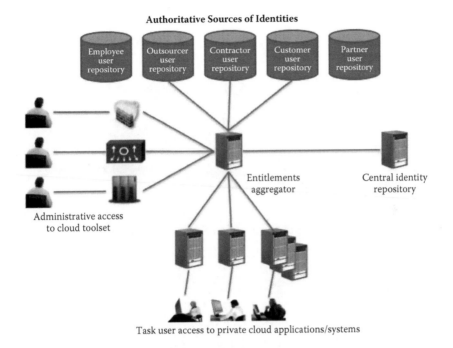

Figure 8.1 Central identity repository architecture.

- Aggregate entitlements information from the layers of cloud administrative consoles, such as your network access, system access, hypervisor access, SAN access, security device access, etc.
- Translate disparate identity and entitlement data into a format that the central identity repository can consume. This constitutes running an extract, transform, load (ETL) process to filter, scope, and validate the integrity of the data consumed.

Building the entitlements aggregator is not a task you want to take lightly. Identity data are triggered differently from repository to repository. You will find that some data sets do not have the flags you require. An example would be that they have "new hire" and "termination" noted in their identity report to you but do not have "transfers" or "leave of absence." These inconsistencies have to be addressed to create a standardized identity user table. You may also run into applications that have no way of integrating with an external system. Lastly, as you work through the various user repositories, you may uncover broken processes that corrupt the integrity of your identity data. You may have to work upstream to change workflows and address problems with departmental cultures. Review the different challenges that are unique to your enterprise and adjust your tact accordingly.

8.3.2 Authoritative Sources of Identities

Access to systems and data is not restricted to employees alone in most organizations today. As noted in the beginning of the chapter, there are nonemployees, offshore resources, business partners, vendors, and many other entities that have legitimate business reasons to access your private cloud environment. Each of these user entities has a way of registering its account within your environment. The goal of centralizing identities begins with identifying the authoritative user sources that are in scope.

- Employee repositories: The best place to go for this is payroll data. Have payroll export relevant employee data to your identity aggregator on a daily basis for new hires, transfers, leave-of-absence employees, and terminations.
- Outsourcers: If you are working with an outsourcing organization, collaborate with its human resource department and your outsourcer IT liaison to import a daily inventory of users who do work on behalf of your company. Again, you need to note new hires, transfers, leaves of absence, and terminations.
- Contractors: If you have contractors in your environment, start by funneling all contractors through a common platform to track application, duration, rates, etc. From there, have that common platform feed your entitlements aggregator the relevant contractor employee data on a daily basis.
- Customers: Your customers pay to use your cloud services. The billing department might be the best place to pull customer identities into your entitlements aggregator. Some of you may have free consumer-based cloud applications. In those cases, it might be better to use identity federation with the likes of Facebook or Google, as opposed to pulling them into your cloud user repository.

- Business partners: Some of you may open up your cloud applications to partners and thus have to maintain their accounts. Work with the business partner's IT department to synchronize user access data.

Your project team needs to work with each one of these identity sources to import the proper identity data into the entitlements aggregator.

8.3.3 Administrative Access

We use the term *administrative access* to differentiate from task level access. Administrative access applies to IT staff that has to log on to administrative consoles across the IT stack to configure, monitor, update, and troubleshoot cloud issues.

You have cloud administrators who log on to the orchestration console to set up automation and workflow. You have system administrators who create and deploy OS templates for virtual server deployments. You have network administrators who manage firewalls, define network segmentation rules, and provide virtual local area networks (VLANs) for the hypervisor farm. You have SAN administrators who maintain the back-end data storage concerns. The list goes on. Each one of these IT layers has authentication and authorization for its portion of the infrastructure. Work with the various teams to see if you can import the user repository elements to an ID&AM solution.

At the minimum, most of these administrative portals have capabilities to integrate with Lightweight Directory Access Protocol (LDAP) or the Active Directory. Our recommendation is to consolidate the administrative logons and force multifactor authentication to gain administrative console access over any parts of your private cloud. The administrative can be managed under one process and in one place. Administrative users should not use their privileged accounts for nonadministrative work.

8.3.4 Task User Access

You have internal and possibly external users with access to your private cloud applications and systems. The cloud orchestration interface also provides your end users with the ability to self-provision computing and storage resources. Each of your private cloud applications may have its own user repository to store its user accounts, or it may integrate into an enterprise directory. Your objective is to work with each cloud application owner to integrate his or her identity data to your entitlements aggregator.

8.3.5 Central Identity Repository

The entitlements aggregator's role is to parse and normalize the identity data from the various sources so that the central identity repository can consume, store, and correlate identity information. The functions of the central identity repository are as follows:

- Correlate the identity and entitlements data provided by the entitlements aggregator to isolate the real-person identity and map it to the various accesses he or she has across your private cloud environment.
- Provide a central point of administration for identity management, including provisioning, de-provisioning, processing transfers, and conducting user recertifications. This centralized provisioning engine could be tied to your cloud orchestration toolset to establish self-service user management capabilities.
- Provide visibility into entitlements to cloud resources—how that access was obtained, who approved the access, and whether the access is appropriate. In a disparate model, you will have to manually collect those data from each disparate system.
- Track and store audit trails around user management.

Deploying the central identity repository is an iterative process. Build a foundational architecture that will allow you to absorb applications, administrative systems, and authoritative sources over time. Be aware of the licensing model and make sure you do not price by connectors. Choose to price by the number of real identities (actual persons) or go for an enterprise unlimited license. Create a repeatable model to systematically migrate the myriad identity stores as well as add new ones. You also need to consider capabilities to extend your private cloud identities into the public cloud (either for cloud bursting or to leverage software as a service (SaaS) or platform as a service (PaaS)). Make sure to adopt open protocols that are cloud-friendly. Consider approaches to authentication, delegation, and authorization. Most public cloud vendors have a way to integrate back to your enterprise identity store.

PART IV

SECURING PUBLIC CLOUDS

The move to public clouds may not be a highly coordinated IT project unlike your private cloud implementation. This is especially true in the software as a service (SaaS) model, where any business unit with purchasing power can sign up for SaaS services without informing your information security department. Next thing you know, your production and nonpublic personal information (NPPI) data are out in the cloud. Your terminated users have access to those data because the user provisioning and de-provisioning are not being controlled or monitored by you. Or the SaaS vendor has a security breach because it is a start-up and has invested minimally in establishing a viable security posture.

Similar scenarios can be painted for platform as a service (PaaS). Anyone with a credit card can sign up for an account. Pockets of your development community could already be in the cloud and running production systems without going through security assessments, code scanning, or quality control. Infrastructure as a Service (IaaS) may be the only deployment model that may not go unnoticed, as it has significant IT implications and costs.

In dealing with public clouds, it is imperative to conduct the appropriate security due diligence on the incumbent provider. This is because there are associated lock-in factors after contract negotiations that may cause you significant time, resources, and money to undo. This section begins by emphasizing the importance of enacting a corporate policy for corporate cloud governance. Once you have a policy, it is crucial to have an enforceable workflow to evaluate cloud providers prior to purchase. The cloud assessment process gives your department the avenue to evaluate the risk exposure of the public cloud request. Next, we will focus on evaluating the security controls made available by the cloud providers as well as how to extend your own security posture into the three different cloud service models: software as a service, platform as a service, and infrastructure as a service. Lastly, we will expand on how to conduct the right level of due diligence based on the criticality of the public cloud initiative.

9

ENTERPRISE CLOUD GOVERNANCE

9.1 Security Exposure of Public Cloud Use

The Cloud Security Alliance (CSA) is one of the leading think tanks around cloud security. Its latest white paper, entitled, "Security Guidance for Critical Areas of Focus in Cloud Computing Version 3,"[1] provides a comprehensive set of guidelines for securing cloud implementations across 14 domains. Additionally, CSA also provides a checklist called the Cloud Control Matrix (CCM) Version 1.2[2] that has 98 rows of control specification to be considered when planning for cloud adoption.

CSA's methodology is completely appropriate for evaluating public cloud providers in the context of significant IT and business transformation projects, such as:

- Migrating traditional IT infrastructure to an infrastructure as a service (IaaS)
- Database team signing up for platform as a service (PaaS) to enable databases in the cloud
- Leveraging cloud storage as an archiving solution
- Creating a cloud-based development and deployment model using a PaaS
- Enabling key corporate functions such as human resources or accounting by subscribing to software as a service (SaaS) providers with specialized and mature functions

It is also important to note that there are instances of public cloud use that are much smaller scale. Examples of these include

- Business users signing up for a specific SaaS application to meet their departmental requirement
- End users signing up for services such as document sharing or calendaring and uploading company data to the cloud

115

- Developers or development team signing up for PaaS to test a new idea
- A business partner requiring your company to use a particular SaaS service for collaboration

From a pragmatic standpoint, you have limited time and resources to evaluate all these cloud endeavors. If you apply the 98 rows of control statements to every cloud service provider (CSP) that your business wants to use, you may need to staff an army of analysts to deal with the volume. Some of your requestors may also be extremely frustrated because they are just trying to sign up for a $5,000 cloud service and you spend 2 months evaluating the security of their CSP. Later in this chapter, we will talk about establishing a cloud approval workflow and applying the right level of rigor to manage the risk of cloud deployments. Right now, let us consider the importance of addressing the uncontrolled expansion of public cloud use in your enterprise (see Table 9.1).

Uncontrolled migration to public cloud severely compromises your ability to uphold your corporate security posture. It is crucial that security become integral to any cloud migration project, be it SaaS, PaaS, or IaaS. Your department needs to evaluate the risk associated with the use of public cloud. Enact a corporate information security policy governing cloud use to regain control over uncontrolled public cloud subscriptions.

9.2 Corporate Cloud Use Policy

Much like the acceptable use policy, the cloud use policy provides guidance for how employees should regard the use of public clouds for company purposes. The policy must be broad enough to cover the entire gamut of use cases, from subscribing to online personal storage to migrating data centers to an IaaS. Enact a security policy that restricts the use of public cloud services without proper approvals. Incorporate this as part of your information security policy so that it has the weight of corporate enforcement. Here is an example of such a policy:

> Any individual or group in the company using external cloud services must first have the cloud provider reviewed and approved by the business

Table 9.1   Security Exposure Due to Cloud Proliferation

SECURITY EXPOSURE	DESCRIPTION
Exposure of sensitive or regulated data	• Confidential data are uploaded to a public SaaS prior to validating the security controls of the provider. • This exposes your organization to the possibility of security breaches that could result in regulatory penalties, reputational damage, notification and settlement costs, and loss of business.
Exposure of intellectual property	• Developers could be uploading company proprietary code onto the public cloud platform. • Loss of intellectual property could compromise the company's competitive edge.
Lack of user access management	• User management in a SaaS is typically done through an administrative portal supplied by the service provider. • The department that owns the relationship with the provider typically manages these user accounts. • There is little or no oversight over role-based access control, user provisioning and de-provisioning, certification, or roles and controls. • Least privilege is not exercised at the user account level, exposing sensitive data to unauthorized users. • Users who have been terminated from the company may still have access to the company's data due to the public cloud portal and the lack of de-provisioning. • Transfers and change of roles are not captured by the user management process, so users that have no business reason to access the cloud service may still be able to do so.
Lack of electronic discovery capabilities to support legal cases	• The majority of the cloud providers are multitenant and may not provide electronic discovery services to the data within their environment because this violates the confidentiality of their other clients. • The lack of electronic discovery could significantly compromise your company's ability to conduct or comply with legal hold requirements. This could result in the loss of cases, further litigation, and other legal penalties.

(continued)

Table 9.1   Security Exposure Due to Cloud Proliferation (continued)

SECURITY EXPOSURE	DESCRIPTION
Compliance issues due to the lack of security controls	• A cloud provider is essentially a third party. Regulations, especially in the financial and healthcare industries, require that you hold third parties responsible for the protection of your data. • Without conducting the proper due diligence on the cloud provider, you are exposed to noncompliance with these regulations. • Noncompliance, depending on its severity, could result in warnings, fines, suspension of rights, and litigation.
Applications published to the Internet without proper quality or security controls	• Weak controls lead to data breaches, rogue control of your Internet presence, and possible web defacement.

executive, the IT executive, and the information security officer positions. Complete the cloud form to start the approval chain.

Each organization's approval chain is different. Some may use an IT architectural board to review the use of cloud. Others may add the CIO, head of compliance, and chief risk officer for the sign-off process. Some may only require sign-off if the cloud use contains nonpublic personal information (NPPI) or intellectual property. If the organization is decentralized, the business division's executive is included in the decision making. The point is to find the right level of endorsement within your organization to give legitimacy to the cloud use policy.

9.3 Cloud Request Form

The cloud use policy must be socialized to the entire organization, especially business, corporate services, IT, and development executives. The policy provides the basis for enforcement and should be incorporated into your information security awareness training. Additionally, incorporate the cloud use policy into your company's procurement process. Train the procurement department to question any public cloud use request and direct it to the information security department prior to final negotiations. Create an intuitive form to kick off the request and work with the requestor to complete the review process. The form should contain the following components:

- Information about the requestor so you can respond to it as well as get some organizational context around the request.
- Ask for the business purpose of the public cloud use. Have the requestor describe the specific purpose and intended value of leveraging cloud computing for its effort/project.
- Ask the requestor to identify the information asset or business function that will reside in the public cloud. Ask for a data flow diagram to better understand how the public cloud will be used and what the interdependencies are.
- Ask the requestor the estimated or allocated capital and operational expenditure for the public cloud project.
- Evaluate the value of the information asset to the company by asking a series of clarifying questions:
  - How would your company be harmed if the asset became widely public and distributed or if the information/data were unexpectedly changed?
  - How would your company be harmed if the asset were unavailable for a period of time or failed to provide expected results?
  - Are there any regulatory or contractual issues that prohibit the information/data from being stored outside your company's secure network?
  - Will your company's NPPI data or intellectual property be stored on the cloud provider's system?
- Ask the requestor what cloud service model it is subscribing to—software as a service, platform as a service, or infrastructure as a service?
- Ask it to provide contact information for the cloud provider as well as any documentation that may help in the evaluation of the public cloud use.

The form can be integrated to your ticketing system or corporate intranet. Fulfillment of the form can take a variety of workflows, depending on your organization and cloud use policy. In a decentralized organization with high security requirements, such as healthcare and finance, there are sometimes business information security managers assigned to each business area.

9.4 Cloud Approval Workflow

Once you enact this policy and publicize the form, you will be bombarded with requests. To fulfill the avalanche of requests, create a cloud approval workflow that provides an easy-to-understand process for your organization to submit its public cloud use requests. The cloud use approval process should have the following attributes:

- **Publicize the workflow and inject enforcement points.** Just because you have a policy does not mean it will be followed. You need to identify how cloud requests are currently being fulfilled and create a gate to funnel all requests through your cloud approval workflow. Work with your procurement department to alert the requestor of the cloud approval process. Go further upstream and socialize the process to department heads within your organization. Post the cloud form and the approval workflow on the corporate intranet. Incorporate the approval process in your mandatory annual security policy training.

- **Clearly define the roles and responsibilities for members of the cloud approval team.** Draw a responsible, accountable, consulted, informed (RACI) chart to identify all the major stakeholders in the cloud approval process. Each company is different due to the varying organizational governance models. You need to clearly define who needs to play what role in your organization for your cloud approval process.

- **Provide notification and status to the requestor.** Leverage an intranet or a SharePoint site to provide real-time status. Otherwise, include in the workflow notification e-mails to the requestor.

- **Have consistent success criteria and a set of final deliverables.** You need to apply the same standards across the different cloud service providers (CSPs) being evaluated. The final deliverables should capture the summary of the request, the risk analysis conducted on the CSP, the recommendations for mitigating controls, and the final approval status.

- **Have a defined service level so that requestors know the lead time they need to allocate for their public cloud project.** You will also need to staff accordingly to meet the service level agreement (SLA). Make sure you create buffer for executive sign-offs, as they may get bogged down and affect your SLA. You can create standing meetings to review these requests with them and have them assign delegates for approvals.

- **Apply the right level of rigor to the different cloud requests.** Cloud initiatives could range from $5,000 to $5M. They also have varying degrees of business impact in the areas of availability and data compromise. You need to develop criteria for applying the right level of due diligence to these various requests to align risk management activities to effort and time spent.

Figure 9.1 shows a sample cloud approval workflow that will work in most organizations.

Your organization may process approvals differently and you may have different steps to your workflow. Embed the criteria for applying the right level of due diligence to the cloud workflow. We recommend putting the cloud use request through three filters.

- **Filter 1—Budget.** The amount of budget allocated is a clear-cut way of estimating how critical this project is to the business. We used $100K as the first cutoff point, but this is an

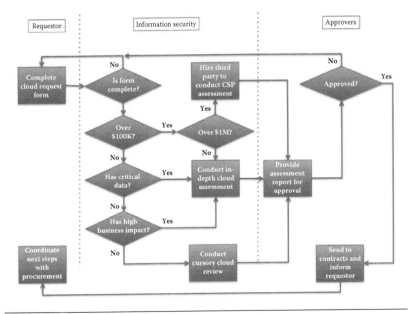

Figure 9.1   Cloud approval workflow for public cloud use policy.

arbitrary number based on your IT spend. The principle here is that you need to draw the first budgetary line to separate out a cursory versus in-depth assessment. We also assigned a second budgetary threshold of $1M to separate out an internal in-depth assessment versus an external consulting cloud assessment engagement. The logic here is that for major cloud transition initiatives, you might want the added value of a specialized consulting firm to put a rubber stamp on your cloud review. A security consulting company that conducts CSP reviews as a business can bring to the selection process experience from reviews completed with other companies, depth of knowledge in cloud assessments, and an unbiased opinion. The final output for the engagement will also provide an audit trail of due care prior to engaging a cloud vendor. A side benefit to this is that you can hold a third party accountable for the quality of the cloud assessment.

- **Filter 2—Data type.** Even if the budget is under the first threshold (in our case $100K), the type of data transacted provides a second filter to push a cursory review to an in-depth assessment. Critical data could cover regulated data, intellectual property, and market-sensitive or competitive information. Data that your company classifies as confidential should be carefully examined before they are pushed to the public cloud.

- **Filter 3—Business impact.** This is a catchall filter for small budgeted cloud projects that are not transacting NPPI data but can affect the business significantly if disrupted or breached. These types of cloud use are few and far between, but they do exist. An example could be a cloud service that is used to conduct analytics of non-NPPI data and send the results to a chain of business-critical services that are hosted internally.

From the request form you should make a determination of whether to use a cursory review, an in-depth cloud assessment, or hire a consulting firm to conduct a thorough CCM (or its equivalent) review. This is dependent on your company's risk appetite, fiscal discipline, and procurement culture, as well as the number of resources you have to conduct these assessments.

References

1. Cloud Security Alliance. Security guidance for critical areas of focus in cloud computing V3.0. Accessed June 28, 2012, https://cloudsecurity-alliance.org/guidance/csaguide.v3.0.pdf.
2. Cloud Security Alliance. Cloud controls matrix V1.2. Accessed June 28, 2012, https://cloudsecurityalliance.org/wp-content/uploads/2011/08/CSA_CCM_v1.2.xls.

10

Cursory Cloud Use Review

10.1 Overview

The objective of the cursory review is to provide a quick turnaround for assessing the numerous requests for cloud services and enforcing security standards on cloud use. Typically these reviews come to you when the business unit has already made its selection and is going through procurement to purchase the cloud service. It will be anxious to push its project forward; hence you need to create a format that can easily facilitate review and approval.

Some prerequisites to consider when processing the cloud use request form:

- Evaluate the data criticality section of the form and review posted corporate security policies regarding controls around the different data types and situations (e.g., public, intellectual property, nonpublic personal information (NPPI), etc.).
- Add areas to your review with the cloud vendor (or request vendor documentation) depending on determined data criticality and requirements around the data. Ensure that you address confidentiality, integrity, and availability that are appropriate for the information in the cloud. Example:
  - Data in the cloud are just compiled code: All areas are reviewed, but not required.
  - Data in the cloud are NPPI data: Serious issues will arise if many advanced requirements are not satisfied.
- Notify the requestor of the progress as the request moves through the evaluation and process.
  - Complete your review and recommendation using a standardized format that covers the following sections:

- The request: Note the business unit or departmental representative that is completing the cloud use form and the request that is being made.
- The asset or data that will reside in the cloud: Describe to the approver what asset is going to reside in the public cloud.
- The impact if that asset or data are lost or stolen: Provide your own estimate of the risk at hand based on your review.
- The protection mechanisms: The summarized output from the documentation review and security interviews conducted with the cloud provider.
- Recommendation: The opinion of the information security department to the approvers regarding the cloud use request. Recommendation may contain conditional approvals with stipulations.
- Approvals: The name of the executive(s) that signed the requests.

- Post your finished review, any approvals (if approved), supporting documentation, and the "summary line" for the Client Information Security Officer (CISO) in a centralized file store (SharePoint, security intranet site, security shared folder, etc.) for auditing purposes.

10.2 Interview with Cloud Service Provider

The actual assessment process involves engaging the point of contact in the requestor section of the cloud use form and arranging interviews with the appropriate parties from the cloud provider's information security or IT teams.

At the minimum, cover the areas in Table 10.1 with the cloud providers.

One piece of advice is to create a short-form version of this question set and send it to the provider prior to your interview with it. This allows for some preparation time and will give it a strong idea of what you are looking for. It also helps the provider gather the right resources within its organization to dialogue with you. The question set is limited due to the cursory nature of your review. Pay attention to its security culture when interviewing the provider and reviewing its documentation.

Table 10.1   Interview with the Cloud Service Provider

CERTIFICATIONS, POLICY, AND ORGANIZATIONAL ADHERENCE	RATIONALE
Is there a country location guarantee, for example, for privacy laws?	If you are subjected to data privacy laws that govern the cross-border transfer of data, you need to vet the cloud provider's practice around data movement and storage.
Does the provider have external security attestations?	Most enterprise-grade providers should conduct an external third-party audit of their security. In the United States, providers often use the Statement on Standards for Attestation Engagements 16 or (SSAE 16; formerly SAS 70 Type II). In Europe, ISO 27001/2 is used. These reports should be available upon request. Make sure to review the control definitions and findings lists.
Review its incident management process.	Clarify the processes for handling security incidents. Establish the roles and responsibilities. Clarify liabilities and service levels for recovery and breach notification.
Does it perform employee background checks? Does it outsource certain functions?	Understand its hiring practices. If it has contractors or outsourcers, ask for clarification on how it vets its resources, maintains limited access, and protects against data leakage.
Ask about business continuity and disaster recovery.	If you are using the cloud provider for a critical or production function, make sure you establish clear business continuity and disaster recovery processes.
AUTHENTICATION AND AUTHORIZATION	RATIONALE
Will the cloud provider do Active Directory (AD) integration?	If yes, push for integration with your Active Directory infrastructure and integrate it into your existing provisioning and de-provisioning processes. If no, work with your account provisioning team to be the keeper of the user management function on the cloud provider's administrative portal. The goal of AD integration is to stop business units from managing cloud users, and closing the gap of terminated employees being able to access company data or functions after their tenure. It also creates a standardized approach to user management.

(continued)

Table 10.1 Interview with the Cloud Service Provider (continued)

Review general access controls: passwords, inactive accounts, lockouts, and terminations, as well as privileged access—vendor side (them) and customer side (us).	Understand the cloud provider's ability to provide appropriate role-based access control and account integrity for its users (them) and its customers (us). Review how it manages entitlements. Review its user provisioning, certification, and monitoring processes.
Does it perform application access logging and correlation?	Understand what monitoring and audit trail capabilities exist for application access. This is needed for detecting rogue behavior or root cause analysis of security incidents.
DATA PROTECTION	**RATIONALE**
What encryption capabilities does the cloud provider have for data in motion?	Validate all capabilities for data-in-motion encryption. The latest version of Secure Socket Layer (SSL) is highly recommended for any company applications in the cloud. Also ensure that it uses the most current SSL capabilities. There is also the option of requesting a site-to-site VPN tunnel between the cloud provider and your company to restrict noncompany sanction access to the cloud portal.
What encryption capabilities does the cloud provider have for data at rest?	Validate all options for database and backup encryption. NPPI data should be encrypted in the cloud. If not NPPI, where possible and not cost- or performance-prohibitive, push for encryption of data. Also ensure that backup tapes are encrypted before being shipped off-site.
How does it manage its encryption keys?	Ask it for its life cycle key management processes. Understand how keys are issued, used, rotated, backed up, recovered, and destroyed.
How is it enforcing least-privileged access to our data?	Validate its security controls around data access. Have it clarify its data protection stance for multitenancy.
What are its data life cycle management policies and processes?	Ensure that your data are securely wiped upon termination of the contract. Also understand its data and log retention policies.
APPLICATION AND HOST LEVEL PROTECTION	**RATIONALE**
What is its patching process like, for example, application, OS, etc.?	Review its patch management process to understand its windows of vulnerability. Ensure that it has a robust patching process for systems, applications, and network devices.

(continued)

11

IN-DEPTH CLOUD ASSESSMENT

11.1 Overview

As noted earlier, if your company is embarking on a major public cloud initiative (such as migration of your production infrastructure to the cloud or leveraging a software as a service (SaaS) for a business core function), conducting the cursory review is insufficient. The depth of the review process has to correspond with the significance of the public cloud use initiative. Per the cloud approval workflow, you should establish a set of defined criteria for when to conduct an in-depth assessment versus a cursory review.

The objective of the in-depth cloud assessment is to provide a thorough and grounded security evaluation of the incumbent cloud service provider (CSP) so that your decision makers can execute their goals while effectively managing the risks of moving to cloud. The senior executives of the company have the right to accept, transfer, or mitigate the risks based on their risk appetite and weighing the upside of going with a certain CSP. Your job is to provide a clear picture of that risk so they can make an informed decision.

In a cloud service model, your security posture is at the mercy of the cloud provider. The precontractual stage is crucial to examining the viability of the CSP's security controls. A thorough and grounded evaluation comes not only from conducting a checkmark assessment, but also from reading between the lines. Use the questions to peel the layers of bureaucratic answers and identify the culture of security within the CSP.

The following areas should be evaluated in your assessment:

- Security governance: Identify the CSP's commitment to information security and how it manages its security posture.
- Data protection: Follow the data flows and evaluate the security controls along the life cycle of the data.

- Security architecture: Validate the actual technical and administrative controls that are deployed in the CSP.
- Application security: Examine the security of the software development life cycle (more specific to SaaS and platform as a service (PaaS)).
- Identity and access management: Carefully vet out the CSP's user management protocols, including that of nonemployees such as contractors, consultants, business partners, etc. Also consider how they will allow you to manage your users accessing the cloud.
- Compliance: Understand the CSP's ability to support your contractual and business obligations around information security.
- Electronic discovery: Understand the CSP's ability to support court procedures of digital discovery, collection, legal holds, and digital forensics.

In each subsection, we will have generic questions for all service models followed by specific queries targeted at SaaS, PaaS, and infrastructure as a service (IaaS), respectively (if applicable). Like the cursory cloud review, the in-depth cloud assessment begins with the cloud request form. After applying the right filter criteria and determining that the request has to be evaluated with the in-depth cloud assessment, engage the requestor to deep-dive on its cloud initiative.

11.2 Interview with the Requestor

In order to effectively secure this endeavor, you need to start by understanding the objectives of the requestor. If it does not have clear requirements, you are going to run into a series of stumbling blocks, especially during the contractual and operational stages. By clarifying the business rationale behind the request, you will be able to effectively negotiate the fine line of risk versus benefits and provide pragmatic options to the requestor.

Before talking to the cloud provider, ask your cloud requestor or business unit the clarifying questions in Table 11.1 about its cloud initiative.

Similar to the cursory review, make sure to create a document repository for your in-depth cloud assessment. Now that you understand

Table 11.1   Requestor Interview

REQUESTOR INTERVIEW	RATIONALE
Who is the executive sponsor of this project? Who is the technical architect? Who are the stakeholders?	Understanding who is backing this cloud request will shape how you conduct the assessment. If you are dealing with a senior executive that is blasé about security, you would need to summon senior executive support to balance the scale. Knowing the technical architect will also add color to how the assessment will be handled. The goal here is to collaborate closely with the key stakeholders from the inception of this initiative to balance risk management and business goals.
What business function is moving to the cloud? What business advantage does it achieve?	There are myriad reasons why the requestor would spend a significant budget on moving to the cloud. If this is about cost savings, you need to be sensitive about pushing security features that add to the requestor's monthly run rates. If this is about features and functionality, you need to be aware of how these new capabilities would impact the overall security posture. The goal here is to shape your discussions with the CSP around what is important to the requestor and find the balance between business strategy and risk management.
Has the cloud vendor been selected?	Typically the requestor or sponsoring executive has a bias toward a CSP by the time it gets to your cloud approval workflow. If the CSP has not been finalized, you might want to use the cursory cloud review to quickly vet the viability of the down-selected list. If the CSP has been chosen, then you can focus on the in-depth cloud assessment. The sooner you know what you are dealing with, the better you can prepare.
Are there detailed data flow mappings between the enterprise and the CSP?	It is imperative that you understand how critical data will move and rest in the cloud environment. Following the data will highlight key systems to review and which ones to scope out. Additionally, dataflow mappings will also bring to light all the connectivity requirements, from the enterprise to the CSP, and potentially partner interfaces. Connections carrying sensitive data require authentication, authorization, and transport security. You will also have an idea of where the data reside to focus on data-at-rest concerns.

(continued)

Table 11.1   Requestor Interview (continued)

REQUESTOR INTERVIEW	RATIONALE
What is the impact to the company if the data are lost or stolen?	The short answer to this question is in the form. During the interview with the requestor, have it elaborate on the business impact by asking it questions around the amount of data that will be stored (NPPI data breach is around $194 per stolen record), the likelihood of potential exploits, and the hourly cost of downtime. You will ultimately formulate your own risk assessment hearing firsthand from the requestor, who will give you a perspective to its priorities and risk appetite.
What is the impact to the business if the cloud provider is compromised or unavailable? What is the uptime requirement for this function?	Understand what your business resiliency requirements are. There is always a price tag associated with continuity and resiliency requirements. Get a pulse on whether the requestor is willing to pay for this.
Who are the users accessing the cloud application?	Clarify the various user groups that will access the functions and data provided by the cloud service and delineate clear lines of roles and responsibilities between each group.

what your requestor is trying to achieve, let us move to validating the security posture of your CSP.

11.3 Security Governance

Probing the cloud vendors on how they run their information security program is a good gauge for the provider's commitment to security (see Table 11.2 for sample questions). Arrange to speak with the information security executive as well as his or her technical security managers.

Security governance questions are especially important in the SaaS and PaaS models where the CSP manages the entire IT stack from application/platform to the physical layer. In the IaaS model, you have more control over the applications, but you are still dependent on the CSP to manage the virtualization stack down to the physical components. The security governance questions are not specific to cloud service models but are targeted to uncover the level of commitment the CSP has toward information security. If it cannot provide any of the documentation you requested around governance, you need to raise a red flag to the requestor. Most CSPs are focused on economies of scale and the bottom line. Security is often an afterthought or a retroactive design based on a breach or customer demands. Some CSPs operate

Table 11.2 Security Governance Interview

SECURITY GOVERNANCE	RATIONALE
Ask the CSP for copies of its corporate information security policies.	Peruse the policy for statements around risk management, data protection, incident response, identity and access management, encryption, and other key areas. Understand the company's position on information security and see if it aligns to yours. If the policy is lackluster and does not provide adequate coverage, this may be telling of the overall security culture of the company.
Ask for an organizational chart of the information security department. Also have it highlight what other security functions are performed by other groups within the organization.	The number of resources dedicated to information security is a key indicator of a company's commitment to security. The departmental reporting lines also reveal how the company views the security function. If the security department rolls up to IT, it views security as a technical function. If it rolls up to the general counsel, then it sees security as an enterprise risk management function. Also observe how many layers down is the security executive from key decision makers of the company.
Ask the CSP to describe its risk management program.	Use the assessment reports as a jumping point to exploring its risk program. Does it have a rigor around assessing and remediating risk? Who is ultimately responsible for information security within the business line? How are information security budget, priorities, and timelines negotiated? What are the key security metrics that are being tracked for the risk management program? How are risk findings and remediation communicated to cloud customers?
How does the CSP screen its employees? How are their roles assigned? Are they aware of information security policies and standards?	Review the CSP's hiring practices to ensure that it conducts background checks, allocates job roles without segregation of duties conflicts, and is committed to a strong information security awareness program.
How does the CSP govern access for contractors, third parties, and outsourced functions?	Validate if the CSP's information security program stretches to cover third parties and business partners that have the ability to affect service or access your data. This is especially important for financial organizations where laws hold you accountable for managing downstream third parties.

a community cloud and build their practice to accommodate more highly regulated industries, such as finance and healthcare. Talking to their information security executive and technical manager should also give you a strong sense of how competent they are.

11.4 Data Protection

11.4.1 Overview

Data are the lifeblood of the modern business. They also happen to be a highly targeted asset for most enterprises. Following the data as they transition from a closed environment to the open cloud is fundamental to assuring your information security posture.

Data have different manifestations in the three cloud service models. In SaaS, data are completely controlled by the CSP. In PaaS, you write the application logic that handles the data, but the CSP controls data security from the platform down to the infrastructure stack. In IaaS, you own the applications and operating systems that the data reside in. The bulk of data protection responsibilities above the hypervisor layer fall on you. Table 11.3 provides a quick illustration of the typical lines of responsibilities drawn between the CSP and your enterprise.

Table 11.3 Cloud Service Models Responsibility Chart

	SAAS	PAAS	IAAS
Your responsibility	• Usage	• Usage	• Usage
		• Application	• Application
		• Data	• Data
			• Platform
			• Operating systems
CSP's responsibility	• Application	• Platform	• Virtualization
	• Data	• Operating systems	• Servers
	• Platform	• Virtualization	• Storage
	• Operating systems	• Servers	• Networking
	• Virtualization	• Storage	• Physical security
	• Servers	• Networking	
	• Storage	• Physical security	
	• Networking		
	• Physical security		

Work with the technical security resource from the CSP to understand the entire life cycle of your critical data under the cloud provider's care.

11.4.2 Data Protection Questions for All Service Models

Since data protection concerns are more aligned to the different service models, there are a few generic questions that apply to all CSPs (Table 11.4).

11.4.3 SaaS Data Protection Questions

Under the SaaS model, data protection is outside your control. You need to pay special attention to how data move in and out of the cloud environment and from your enterprise. Understand how data are comingled with the other tenants of the CSP as well as clarify any potential connectivity to other partner services (see questions in Table 11.5).

Table 11.4 General Data Protection Questions

DATA PROTECTION	RATIONALE
Have the CSP describe the physical locations of data storage (include geographic locations of data replications and off-site storage).	The physical location of the data may have implications on the legal jurisdiction affecting those data. For example, if a British company places its NPPI data in a U.S. CSP, what laws would the data be subjected to? What if the CSP replicates those data to China? Would the data now be subjected to laws from three different countries? If the data protection laws are not compatible in these three countries, which legal jurisdiction should take precedence? These are key questions that have to be vetted out with your legal department based on the physical data storage locations of the CSP.
Have the CSP identify groups or individuals that have physical and logical access to the physical data storage locations.	Regardless of the service model, key CSP administrators can logically and physically access the SAN or network-attached storage (NAS) of a cloud provider. Understand the access control and logging of such access.

Table 11.5   SaaS Data Protection Questions

SAAS DATA PROTECTION	RATIONALE
Have the CSP map out data flows from the enterprise to the CSP and to potential third parties. Have the CSP describe the data life cycle—import/creation, use, rest, backup, and destruction.	If you are storing NPPI, intellectual property, or business-sensitive data in the public cloud, ensure that you understand the full life cycle of the data flow. Identify areas of vulnerabilities and drill down on security controls in those areas. Follow the entire life cycle of the data from initial import or creation to use to storage to backup tapes and finally, to destruction.
Have the CSP describe data protection controls to ensure appropriate access and separation between tenants.	Focus on administrative, application, and database access. Prioritize by analyzing targets that have the ability to move the most amounts of data. Have the CSP delineate how it controls its database and system administrators in particular. Are there any database monitoring tools? Do they have data leakage prevention (DLP) to detect movement of sensitive data? Also understand how the CSP separates data access per tenant. Does it use logical or physical separation? Does it use encryption domains with different keys per tenant?
Have the CSP delineate encryption capabilities for data at rest and data in motion.	Following the data flow exercise, have the CSP describe encryption capabilities when moving or storing data. Does it use the latest version of SSL and disable use of earlier/less secure versions? Does it offer cell space, table space, or fabric encryption? What cryptographic modules are used? Ensure that they comply to the Federal Information Processing Standards (FIPS 140-2).* Are there additional charges for employing encryption services? Is there a performance impact to the application?
Have the CSP define encryption life cycle key management processes.	Validate how keys are created, protected, used, stored, recovered, and destroyed. On SSL, validate what the CSP's SSL renewal procedures are. If it uses client certificates for two-factor authentication, you need to review its certificate management procedures as well.
Have the CSP discuss the issue of data portability. Cover onboarding and off-boarding of your company's data into the SaaS service.	Ensure the security of the initial data import. Review the CSP's onboarding processes for potential risks. Ensure that data are appropriately accessed and cleaned up from test and intermediate environments. Also discuss an exit strategy with both your business unit or requestor and the CSP. Know what to expect if and when it's time to bring the entire data set back in-house. Set stipulations in the contract to protect your data.

* Information Technology Library for NIST, "FIPS PUB 140-2 Security Requirements for Cryptographic Modules," accessed June 28, 2012, http://csrc.nist.gov/publications/fips/fips140-2/fips1402.pdf.

Table 11.6 PaaS Data Protection Questions

PAAS DATA PROTECTION	RATIONALE
Have the CSP clearly delineate the lines of data protection responsibilities within its PaaS environment.	Depending on the PaaS, there are a range of service offerings that can be consumed within a PaaS solution. Most PaaSs tie their development platform with auto-hosting capabilities where you can publish your applications immediately. Others allow you to publish your applications but have the databases tie in to a different database as a service provider. You need to establish a responsible, accountable, consulted, informed (RACI) chart to identify who is responsible for what when it comes to protecting your critical data.
Work with your requestor and the CSP to understand the data flows in the context of the PaaS.	The difference around data mapping in the SaaS model is that the CSP has absolute control over the data movement and storage. In the PaaS model, you typically have options on how you want the data to flow. PaaS vendors can provide database platforms for you to store your data. You can choose to back-end the data to a hybrid, private cloud or a different PaaS. Work with your requestor and the CSP to map out exactly what the data flow will look like. Once you know where the data are going, you can examine the security controls around their movement and storage.
Understand the encryption offerings or interoperability available with the PaaS provider.	Some PaaS providers offer encryption solutions within their packaged offering. Others may even allow interfacing with your key management capabilities. Drill down with the CSP on what its encryption offerings are. Vet out its key management life cycle processes as well. Your best option is to be able to leverage its encryption capabilities but manage the keys within your environment. That would provide significant data protection from CSP administrators because they do not have the authority to decrypt any data that you have encrypted.

11.4.4 PaaS Data Protection Questions

Under the PaaS model, you are responsible for the application logic protecting your data. However, you are still dependent on the CSP's security for the entire stack below the platform, including OS, hypervisor, and storage area network (SAN) security. Your data might also reside in a MYSQL, MS SQL, or Oracle PaaS, where the CSP's back-end access to these cloud platforms has significant impact to your data security (see questions in Table 11.6).

Table 11.7   IaaS Data Protection Questions

IAAS DATA PROTECTION	RATIONALE
Have the CSP describe what encryption capabilities are available and what they can support.	Inquire to see if the IaaS is able to support encrypting the virtual layer. One of the most effective ways of protecting your data in the cloud is to encrypt the entire virtual stack and manage the keys within your enterprise. If the IaaS vendor has the ability to support this capability, make sure to work with your requestor to build this into the project. Also ensure that you establish encryption for inter- and intracloud communication.

11.4.5 IaaS Data Protection Questions

In the IaaS model, you are mainly responsible for the entire stack minus that which is below the hypervisor layer. You manage your own operating systems and databases, provide application security over your data, and deploy data encryption standards for transport and storage. The CSP has access to the hypervisor layer, so it can see traffic traversing through the physical and virtual switches. It also has access to the SAN storage to peer into your data. Outside of that, you are responsible for applying the same level of rigor over data protection as you did prior to the cloud move (see Table 11.7 questions).

11.5 Security Architecture

Security architecture deals with controls below the platform stack so they will apply to the three service models: SaaS, PaaS, and IaaS. The intent of this question set is not to cover every possible security architecture question about cloud. Giant questionnaires slow the procurement processes down and cause participants to lose faith in the process. Focus on asking the important lead-in questions that will reveal whether the CSP's security is designed into the solution from the ground up or if it is merely an afterthought. Review the CSP's security architecture layer by layer. Use the questions in Table 11.8 to determine the cloud provider's commitment to sound security architecture.

Table 11.8 Security Architecture Questions

SECURITY ARCHITECTURE	RATIONALE
Have the CSP describe how the network is segmented. Have it differentiate physical from logical segmentation.	Understand the controls between network tiers. Ensure that they separate the web-facing tiers from the application and database segments. In the PaaS and IaaS models, understand what controls you have to segment your own network. Discuss how tenants are segmented from each other. Ensure that the environment is segmented enough such that other tenants do not have the ability to impact your end user experience when they need compute, memory, or disk space. Ask for the CSP's firewall management and audit procedures. Also ask about how it separates management traffic from production traffic. Are there choke points to strictly limit administrative access? Can production segmentation be bypassed by jumping on the management and backup virtual local area networks (VLANs)?
Validate if the cloud provider can limit access to the cloud application to your company's subnet or through site-to-site virtual private network (VPN).	This takes your application off the grid and will only access through your corporate network. Some CSPs have the ability to limit your portion of cloud access strictly to your corporate network. This will also act as a safety net to prevent rogue access over the Internet from employees who have left your company but the user de-provisioning for the cloud account was not completed correctly.
How are network threat monitoring, detection, and prevention implemented?	Have the CSP describe its intrusion detection and prevention system (IDS/IPS) deployment. Understand the nodes that are fed into the Security Information Event Manager (SIEM). Have it describe how it handles and addresses security alerts. Ask it about DDoS protection. Ask it about malware protection at the network and host levels. If its threat intelligence architecture is mature, ask it what it offers in terms of tying its security alerts into your SIEM. The goal is to get threat visibility for your cloud systems. In the IaaS model, find out if you have to use what the CSP provides or if you can provision your own threat monitoring virtual appliances in your cloud farm.
Understand the CSP's patch management processes for all flavors of operating systems, network devices, key applications, and the VM infrastructure.	Drill down on how patching is done within the CSP. What is the frequency of patches? How long is the time between patch release and patch deployment? Who makes the decision on patching? What is the rollback procedure if the patch fails? Will the patching activity impact performance, or is there a rolling patch process to ensure uptime while patching?

(continued)

Table 11.8   Security Architecture Questions (continued)

SECURITY ARCHITECTURE	RATIONALE
Have the CSP describe its host level security, from OS hardening to local security policies and security software on the hosts.	Ensure that its servers, VM guest machines, and physical VM clusters are hardened in accordance to published hardening guidelines found in National Institute of Standards and Technology (NIST) and SANS publications.
	Whether it is using an imaging process or VM templates to deploy servers, ensure that its base configuration has the appropriate password controls, local machine policies, default configuration edits, and host protection software. Pay special attention to its bastion host configuration for Internet-facing systems for the SaaS and IaaS models. In the IaaS model, vet out the standard VM image deployment to ensure that its vanilla OS install meets your hardening requirements.
Discuss the CSP's abilities to scale and be resilient in minor and major failures.	Availability is a key principle in information security. Ensure that the cloud provider has the ability to scale to your peak traffic usage without disrupting usability. Explore its ability to failover in the event of hardware, software, and other unexpected failures. Ensure that the CSP can meet your recovery time objectives (RTOs). Also request for the CSP's business continuity plans (BCPs) and disaster recovery (DR) test reports. If it does not have BCPs or has never done any DR testing, you might want to raise concerns to our requestor or business unit.

11.6 Application Security

11.6.1 Overview

Application security is the different per service model. In SaaS, the CSP is fully responsible for the application life cycle. In PaaS, you are responsible for the actual code, but the software development platform and below are owned by the CSP. In IaaS, you are fully responsible for your own application security. We will address each service model individually.

11.6.2 SaaS Application Security

SaaS providers are responsible for the entire SDLC of their code. Carefully go through this section with them to identify their best practices around secure code development and deployment (see Table 11.9 for questions).

Table 11.9   SaaS Application Security Questions

APPLICATION SECURITY	RATIONALE
Have the CSP describe the architecture of its cloud application. Is it using service-oriented architecture or the traditional web application model?	Validate that the application is properly segmented and that data store is not explicitly exposed to the Internet. Examine the connectivity requirements of the application architecture. Verify if the applications publish or consume from other web services. Validate that connectivity to the application is properly authenticated and authorized (be it from a user, another service, or an application).
Have the CSP describe the security elements of its software development life cycle (SDLC).	Does the CSP train its developers on secure coding practices? Does it abide by the guidelines set forth in the Open Web Application Security Project (OWASP)? Does it conduct code review that includes validating security components? Does it scan its code for security vulnerabilities prior to production release? How are security flaws handled? Does it have a process to vet the security and reliability of its shared libraries? If the CSP does not have any form of security in its SDLC, you should raise a major red flag to the requestor.
Have the CSP delineate how it protects its code prior to release as well as its release procedures.	Understand who has access to the code repository and how this access is tracked. Is there a way to contaminate the code prior to production? Are the proper role-based access controls applied to the code repository and the code release processes? Do developers have access to the production environment?

11.6.3 PaaS Application Security

In the PaaS model, your concern is around how the CSP manages the platform stack for development, the security around its code repository, and the controls around application publishing and the runtime environment (see Table 11.10 for questions).

11.7 Identity and Access Management

11.7.1 Overview

Validating the state of identity and access management is fundamental to the protection of data and availability. Two types of identity and access management need to be covered.

Table 11.10   PaaS Application Security Questions

APPLICATION SECURITY	RATIONALE
Have the CSP describe the security components of its code development platform.	Begin with vetting who has access to your segment of the development platform outside of your authorized users. Can CSP administrators log on to your cloud development portal? If so, what types of monitoring are there to prevent code tampering? Are their shared libraries from a reliable and trusted source? Do they have security code scanning tools that can be used during the development process? If not, can they scan your code during preproduction? Can they incorporate your code scanning product or vendor (if you have one)?
Have the CSP describe the protection around its code repository.	What are the processes around code check-ins and build integration? Who else has access to the code repository? What logging exists to track changes to the code repository?
Have the CSP describe its code publishing practices.	What are the controls around code versioning? Does the platform support role-based access control to segregate developers, testers, production support, etc.? Ensure that you know the avenues on how code can be pushed to production, as this could affect your customers, business reputation, and ultimately, revenue.
Have the CSP describe how it securely manages its runtime environments.	Does the platform provide application security monitoring during runtime? Can it detect anomalous web and database access traffic during runtime? Verify the security toolset available to you in the PaaS offering.

- CSP identities: These tie back to administrators and CSP staff and resources that have access to systems, VM, and infrastructure components.
- Customer identities: These are user accounts associated with the application that the SaaS is hosting for their various tenants, including you.

11.7.2 Identity Access Management for CSP Staff

The identity access module applies to the three different service models. CSPs have the following access:

- IaaS, PaaS, SaaS
  - Access to physical data centers
  - Access to data center operations suite of tools
  - Console access to servers, SAN, security tools, and network devices

- - Administration access to the virtualization and orchestration technologies
- PaaS and SaaS
  - Access to development platform, including code repository
  - Administrative access to presentation layer
  - Administrative access to middleware
  - Administrative access to database layer
- SaaS
- Administrative access to applications

The identity access problem is complex. It is not enough to validate employee access. You have a plethora of access cross-pollinated with a range of employees and nonemployees. You need to ask how the CSP provisions contractors, consultants, outsourcers, offshore resources, auditors, business partners, and essentially anyone that could obtain access to its network, systems, databases, and applications. To add to that complexity, you may also have to address the issues of authentication and authorization for interapplication connections and cloud services. (See Table 11.11 for identity and access management questions for CSP staff.)

11.7.3 Identity and Access Management for CSP Customers

Identity management for CSP customers can be loosely categorized into two general areas:

- Task workers: Users in your organization that consume the CSP services, whether applications, platform, or compute services.
- Administrative access: Users within your organization that are given an administrative console to assign rights and manage users, procure or discontinue cloud services, monitor usage and operational metrics, etc.

Adoption models for identity management for cloud services can be done in three modes:

- Local CSP user repository: Accounts are hosted and stored on the CSP's directory services and are typically managed by you via a user administrative console provided by the CSP.

Table 11.11   Identity and Access Management Questions for CSP Staff

IDENTITY AND ACCESS MANAGEMENT	RATIONALE
Have the CSP describe its user provisioning, de-provisioning, transfers, and certification process for its operating systems, databases, network, and applications.	This question focuses on how it manages identities for operational responsibilities of the cloud service. How does it assign different IT roles? How are administrators monitored? How soon are accounts disabled after an employee has been terminated? How does it know that it has disabled access to all applications and systems that the user had? What is the time period for disabling and deleting inactive user accounts? How does it protect the initial distribution of credentials?
What is the identity management process for nonemployees such as contractors, consultants, outsourcers, offshore resources, business partners, etc.?	Financial, healthcare, and payment card industries hold companies responsible for managing their third parties with access to sensitive data and systems. You in turn have to hold your third parties responsible for how they manage nonemployees. Ask the CSP for its third-party management policies and standards. If it does not have any, ask it for specific procedures around how nonemployees are vetted prior to being given access. Go through the identity life cycle to ensure that there are no gaping holes to third-party access. Pay special attention to how these accounts are disabled because third parties do not usually send daily or periodic HR feeds to the CSP to inform it of nonemployee status.
Validate that the CSP has proper controls for its administrative accounts.	Identify the CSP administrator accounts that could severely impact your business function in the cloud. Query how these accounts are provisioned, certified, monitored, and deleted. Do they require multifactor authentication to access administrative rights? Are the access rights loose, or do they restrict the administrators to their required job functions? Do Database Administrators (DBAs) have free rein over your data? Can they move data without being traced? Can administrators cover their tracks by deleting logs? Is there any use of generic accounts?
Validate the CSP's use of service, tests, and application accounts.	How does the CSP manage nonhuman access? Does it have a password-safe or dual-knowledge process for creating, storing, and retrieving critical system credentials? Does it have controls to ensure that nonhuman accounts are not known and cannot be used?

Table 11.12 Identity and Access Management Questions for CSP Customers

IDENTITY AND ACCESS MANAGEMENT	RATIONALE
Validate to see if the CSP's user access management can be extended to your existing enterprise user repository.	The best way to control access to the cloud user accounts is to integrate the authentication back to your enterprise user store. This way, you do not have to re-create user management processes specific to the cloud vendor. You build the connector once and leverage your existing process to manage the users. Some CSPs can integrate directly with you, while others require a cloud identity broker. If the CSP cannot integrate with your user repository, consider leveraging your user provisioning team to manage the cloud user portal. This enables you to have a single point of accountability for user accounts in your enterprise. Do not make the mistake of handing the reins of user provisioning to the requestor's business unit. Make sure to work through the entire identity management life cycle with the CSP.
Validate the CSP's capability for role-based access control.	Ensure that you go through the exercise of working with the requesting business unit to define clear roles and responsibilities. Ensure that the CSP's role-based access control can enforce your segregation of duties rules. In the PaaS model, ensure that there is separation between development and production support. Also be sure to separate task workers from administrators.
Validate if the CSP has support for multifactor authentication around administrative accounts.	Administrative accounts have the ability to significantly impact your security posture. Some CSPs support this capability natively, while others can integrate with a cloud identity broker that has a multifactor authentication feature. We highly recommend enforcing strong authentication and monitoring on your administrative access.

- Integration with your enterprise user repository: The CSP has the ability to integrate back into your enterprise directory to facilitate single sign-on.
- Federated through cloud identity brokers: Cloud identity brokers build integration tools to act as the conduit between various CSPs and your enterprise directory.

See Table 11.12 for identity and access management questions.

11.8 Compliance

Financial, healthcare, and retail organizations have stringent information security compliance requirements. These demands become even more complex when they are migrated to the cloud due to the lack of visibility, control, and accountability. More often than not, compliance becomes a barrier of entry for public cloud adoption. The cost of compliance is also a major hurdle for most companies. If you have to hold a number of cloud vendors accountable for your compliance requirements, you have to throw resources and time at each vendor to conduct audits, follow up on findings, and report on their compliance. Consortiums and vendors alike are pursuing the holy grail of cloud compliance. The two noteworthy intercloud compliance efforts to date are

- CSA's CloudTrust Protocol
- RSA's Cloud Trust Authority

The Cloud Security Alliance (CSA) supports the CloudTrust Protocol.[1] In its own words, "The CloudTrust Protocol (CTP) is the mechanism by which cloud service consumers ask for and receive information about the elements of transparency as applied to cloud service providers."[2] To simplify, CTP provides a standard protocol for cloud users to consistently request assertions, evidence, and affirmations from participating CSPs. This allows the cloud customer to efficiently evaluate the state of compliance for the CSP and compare it to others. The challenge of CTP is to gain enough adoption from major cloud providers to become a true industry standard.

Another response to the compliance problem is being broached by RSA with the advent of the Cloud Trust Authority. RSA's Cloud Trust Authority is essentially a cloud intermediary with a suite of security services, such as identity management and compliance profiling. Similar to CloudTrust, the success of RSA's Cloud Trust Authority hinges on adoption from major cloud providers to open their kimono up to RSA to be assessed.

Both CloudTrust Protocol and Cloud Trust Authority signal an important trend for a standardized compliance approach to public cloud adoption. However, these are still early days for both approaches, and you are still responsible for holding the CSP accountable for abiding with your compliance requirements (see Table 11.13 for sample compliance questions).

Table 11.13 Compliance Questions

COMPLIANCE	RATIONALE
Ask the CSP for the last two copies of all external security audits.	Two reports give you a comparison of their findings and ability to remediate over time. Ask to read the CSP's Statement on Standards for Attestation Engagements 16 (SSAE 16) in the United States or the International Standard on Assurance Engagements 3402 (ISAE 3402) outside the United States reporting for their data centers. An alternative is to request its ISO 27001/2 certification report. Review these third-party reports and evaluate the control objectives of the CSP. Make sure they match up with your compliance requirements. If you have Payment Card Industry (PCI) compliance requirements, ask the CSP for its report of compliance for PCI-DSS. If it is unwilling to provide soft copies, tell them that you will view the reports in person or through an online-sharing session so you cannot retain copies of their sensitive reports.
Ask the CSP for external penetration testing or vulnerability assessment reports.	Ask it for the last two copies of its penetration tests or vulnerability assessment reports. Validate that it tracks and remediates critical findings.
Have the CSP explain its process to accommodate an on-site audit from your company.	You need to add the right-to-audit clause in your contract and work with the CSP to establish an audit process. Provide your entire control statement to the CSP at the inception of the relationship and establish a time frame for periodic audit.
Validate with the CSP what compliance reporting it will provide to you.	CSPs that have highly regulated customers should be familiar with the process of providing compliance reporting on a periodic basis. Establish the parameters within the compliance reporting, the frequency of the report, and the secure delivery of the contents.

11.9 Electronic Discovery

Your company has legal obligations to abide by the Federal Rules of Civil Procedure when it comes to acquiring, preserving, and presenting electronic evidence. You probably have deployed e-mail archiving, digital forensics, and electronic discovery capabilities within your enterprise to accommodate your legal department's demands. When your data sit in the cloud, you are still required to comply with the same electronic discovery proceedings. You need to establish the cost and capabilities of electronic discovery with your CSP. See Table 11.14 for electronic discovery questions.

Table 11.14   Electronic Discovery Questions

ELECTRONIC DISCOVERY	RATIONALE
Have the CSP describe its electronic discovery procedures in a multitenant environment.	In the event of a legal matter involving data that are stored with the cloud provider, what procedures are available to you as a customer to comply with the Federal Rules of Civil Procedure governing electronic data? Establish service level agreements and the cost considerations up front. Validate with your CSP whether your discoverable data are isolated or shared with other tenants. Make sure you are clear that the CSP knows how to conduct a proper electronic discovery request, including collection of artifacts, maintaining chain of custody, and preserving the integrity of the data collected.
Have the CSP describe its legal hold procedures.	There might be instances where your company is required to place legal holds on certain classes of data. Does the CSP have a well-defined procedure to execute legal holds on your behalf? What is the cost of that? Are there procedures to migrate the electronic data in question to your legal department or outside counsel while preserving its integrity?
Clarify with the CSP what its data retention rules are and how it deletes the data upon the end date of that rule.	Establishing and enforcing a robust retention policy may limit data from being used against your company once they have been deleted. Work with your legal department to ensure that the CSP has the ability to comply with your data retention rules.

11.10 Closing the Loop

The final output of your cloud assessment is a report containing findings and recommendations for senior executives to deliberate over the cloud decision. On your in-depth cloud assessment final report, make sure to include the following topics:

- Executive overview: Provide a high-level summary and risk rating for the CSP in question.
- Prioritized security stipulations: Based on the interviews with the CSP, provide clear recommendations on what must be included in the contract. Include cost implications.
- Section breakdown: Provide a write-up for each subsection (security governance, data protection, security architecture, and so on) and expand on how the security stipulations were derived.

If the senior executives agree to push this through, then work with your legal and procurement team to negotiate and redline the master service agreement, service level agreement, statement of work, and other corresponding contracts, to include the security stipulations.

References

1. Accessed from https://cloudsecurityalliance.org/research/ctp/.
2. Accessed from http://assets1.csc.com/cloud/downloads/wp_cloudtrust-protocolprecis_0730 10.pdf.

Third-Party Cloud Assessment

12.1 Overview

For major cloud projects, our recommendation is to select a reputable cloud assessor vendor (CAV) to conduct the security assessment and provide you with its findings and recommendations. The benefits of using this approach are as follows:

- Methodology: CAVs build their program on industry standards.
- Expertise: Successful CAVs staff subject matter experts in this field and build practical experience from their diverse engagements. Some may have the ability to provide benchmark data. Additionally, your staff can focus on your core business as opposed to being pulled to run the cloud assessment.
- Credibility: Select a CAV that has a reputation to uphold. The brand name of the CAV will also lend credibility to the assessment in the eyes of senior executives and auditors.
- Efficiency: CAVs may already have reviewed the cloud service provider (CSP) in question or have proper relationships within the CSP to get answers quicker and with more accuracy.
- Recourse: Using a CAV transfers the liability of the assessment to it. In the wake of a significant security incident in the CSP, you may have legal recourse on the CAV for not providing the proper due diligence.

There are some disadvantages to hiring a CAV:

- Cost: This is the obvious one, as you have to pay an engagement fee for bringing a CAV onboard. There is an intangible offset to this cost, as you would be using your own resources regardless.
- Objectivity: CAVs may have biases toward CSPs due to business relationships. However, this is a fine line because they

have to uphold their reputation. The other side of the coin is that the CAV may skew the assessment to sell more work (remediation and delivery engagements are good follow-up candidates to an assessment).

• Dependency: You are not building knowledge capital and experience if the review was passed on to a CAV. Also, the relationships with key members of the CSP that could have been built during the review process would be lost to the CAV.

The pros outweigh the cons, and you need to make the right decision on whether to bring in a CAV or not depending on your corporate context and priorities.

12.2 Selecting an Assessor

Not all CAVs are created equally. Naturally, there are a number of factors that make one CAV better than another to work with your organization. The factors in Table 12.1 should be considered during the CAV selection process.

The U.S. government recently enacted the Federal Risk and Authorization Management Program (FedRAMP) to facilitate the review of CSPs for government use. It has a process around selecting third-party assessment organizations (3PAOs) that follows the NIST 800-53 guidelines to evaluate CSPs. Only CSPs that are authorized by FedRAMP can be used by government agencies. If you trust the vetting process of FedRAMP, this may be a shortcut for selecting your CAVs. To date, there are nine 3PAOs that have gone through the FedRAMP accreditation process.

12.3 Finalizing the SOW

Once you have down-selected to your CAV of choice, go through the statement of work (SOW) to lock down deliverables, time frames, and pricing. Generally, you have the option of going with fixed price or time and materials (T&M). Table 12.2 lists the pros and cons of both approaches in the context of a cloud security assessment.

The cloud security assessment is a defined process with clear deliverables. We highly recommend going for a fixed-price engagement

Table 12.1   Selecting a Cloud Assessment Vendor

SELECTION CRITERIA	DESCRIPTION
Review the CAV's cloud security assessment methodology.	Have the CAV describe its cloud security assessment framework. Have its describe approaches, processes, end deliverables, and assessment tools (if used). Ask the CAV if its methodology is aligned to industry standards such as CSA's Cloud Control Matrix or NIST SP 800-53. Ask for samples of its assessment questionnaires.
Ask for references of recent cloud security assessment clients (preferable if they are from within your industry silo).	Get an idea of the number of cloud security assessments the CAV has conducted. This is a relatively new field, so the number might be small. Look for CAVs that have performed assessments for a client in your industry or whether the assessment was on the same CSP you need to review. Ask for names of contacts so that you can call on them as references.
Ask to review some sample reports.	Review the sample reports to ensure that they align to your set of requirements for the assessment. They will also shed light on the quality of the CAV's assessment.
Evaluate the credentials of the CAV's assessors.	Ask for some sample resumes of their cloud security assessors. If possible, ask to interview the potential candidate that the CAV will staff on your project if it wins the statement of work (SOW).
Have the CAV describe its pricing models.	Work with the CAV to determine what it needs from you to price your engagement. Once you provide the data to it, have the CAV provide some budgetary pricing back to you. Understand the elements of its pricing package.
Estimate the CAV's reputation in the marketplace as a trusted advisor.	Review the CAV's financials in regards to work done in the security practice. Is this a side business for its organization, or is it the CAV's bread and butter? Is the CAV known in the industry? Has it been reviewed or rated by major IT research firms (such as Gartner or Forrester)? Also, reach out to your own peers to inquire about the credibility of the CAV.

with the CAV where possible. Typically, fixed-price models indicate that the CAV has a mature process for conducting its assessments and can leverage repeatable processes. Make sure you spend the time to clearly define your success criteria and the deliverables you expect out of the fixed-price engagement. If you capture this incorrectly, there will be little flexibility to change your scope without incurring penalties. Establish a pay schedule that corresponds to a phased delivery if you expect the project to take more than a few weeks. Make sure you clarify if the fixed price covers the costs of travel and expenses. If it does not, make sure you allocate a limit on the travel and expense

Table 12.2   Fixed Price versus Time and Materials

ENGAGEMENT PRICING	PROS	CONS
Fixed price	Predictable cost of engagement. Defined success criteria. Efficient because CAV will not prolong the engagement. Coverage for unforeseen complexity that is within the scope of the success criteria.	CAV may cut corners to capitalize on the fixed price. Inflexible: Scope additions that are not captured in the initial SOW will require an amendment and extra cost.
Time and materials (T&M)	Provide flexibility to the engagement and allow for scope change without contract revisions. Easy comparison for the work performed, as you can compare hourly or daily rates between CAVs.	The CAV is not incented to complete the work efficiently, and you may be billed for unexpected hours. Unpredictable capital expenditure.

costs. Check the quality of the work, as the CAV is incented to finish the job quickly. Reserve the right to sit in on some of the interview processes to audit the work.

Only use T&M if you need to incorporate flexibility into the engagement. Make sure to incorporate a weekly status from the CAV to account for the hours spent and the work completed. You might want to create checkpoints to go over findings and track their progress.

12.4 Closing the Loop

Once the deliverables have been turned over by the CAV, walk through the report with your cloud engagement decision makers. Similar to the in-depth cloud assessment, present the prioritized findings of the CSP and weigh in on the stipulations to be incorporated in the CSP contract.

PART V
SECURING MOBILE

Mobility is the other IT revolution that is changing the way we work and live. The advent of smart phones and tablets has stretched the perimeter of the enterprise and limits our ability to fully control the endpoint. Additionally, the business culture around mobile devices has changed. The advancement of apps, the growth of the social network, and the quality of phone cameras have together blurred the lines between work and play. Personal data are stored alongside company information assets. "Bring your own device" is becoming more prevalent. Select departments, marketing and sales in particular, are equipping their workforce with iPads. Retail stores are taking payments with smart phones. This is a new era of mobility.

In this section, we will look at the current mobility landscape and methods to secure it. First, we will consider the security around your mobile infrastructure. We will start by examining the major mobile architectures—RIM and Microsoft in particular. We then move on to an in-depth look at mobile clients and their connection to your enterprise applications, as well as downloading and using third-party mobile applications. We will look at iPhone 3GS (and later), Windows Phone 7, Android (2.3 and later), as well as BlackBerry Enterprise Server. We will look at your mobile endpoints, breaking down some common struggles and offering a few suggestions regarding how to secure them. Lastly, we'll touch on the development of secure mobile applications in your organization, as well as your Enterprise App Store/Google Play setup.

In this section, we will discuss the viability of different vendors serving the mobile space. The disclaimer is that we are merely giving our point of view as practitioners who have had to examine different market offerings to address some of our own challenges with mobility. The opinions on vendors are point in time and perfunctory. Please conduct your own due diligence as the mobile security market is a dynamic space.

13

MOBILE SECURITY INFRASTRUCTURE

13.1 Overview

Since your mobility infrastructure is composed of mostly servers, you must be diligent with regard to patching. You must keep systems hardened and perform regular environment reviews and upgrades as required. Verizon's "2012 Data Breach Investigations Report" provides some eye-opening statistics:

- 97% of breaches were avoidable through simple or intermediate controls.
- 96% of attacks were not highly difficult.
- 94% of all data compromised involved servers.[1]

What does this mean to you? It means that a small but consistent level of due diligence on your part with regard to patching and configuration adjustments translates into a significant drop in breaches into your mobility infrastructure made ridiculously easy by something like missing patches.

13.2 BlackBerry® Enterprise Server Architecture

In an effort to simplify their infrastructure and reduce their support profile, more enterprises will move away from the once popular BlackBerry Enterprise Server infrastructure and migrate toward Exchange ActiveSync plus a mobile device management (MDM) infrastructure; the MDM will help you more granularly manage your mobile users. There will continue to be Blackberry Enterprise Server BES strongholds, such as government-related entities, and other high-security businesses that work with them, but many we have talked to over the last couple of years complain about the extra work or cost

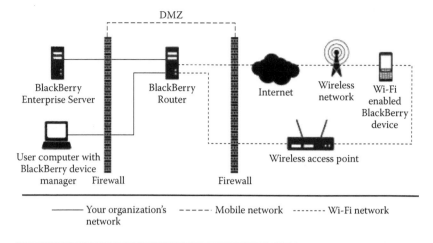

Figure 13.1   From Research in Motion Limited, "BlackBerry Enterprise Server: Placing the BlackBerry Router in the DMZ," accessed April 7, 2012, http://docs.blackberry.com/en/admin/deliverables/25734/Blackberry_Enterprise_Server-Security_Note--1395142-0307061517-001-5.0.3-US.pdf.

incurred with using BlackBerry products. BlackBerry devices require their own infrastructure in addition to what you have already set up for your existing e-mail infrastructure. Also, it requires someone on staff with specific knowledge of the BlackBerry device setup, who is (hopefully) keeping up with the recommended improvements on both the software and hardware side. Knowledge of the setup will become academic for many of us, but it's still worth covering a few points.

Your secure BlackBerry devices won't be that secure without a secure setup. Even though you may have your BlackBerry Router in your demilitarized zone (DMZ), you must still ensure that your BlackBerry Enterprise Server is not directly accessible from the Internet (Figure 13.1). The advantage to having a BlackBerry Router is that if it is compromised, it does not store or transfer device transport keys.[2] You can simply replace it, of course, after thoroughly examining the reason(s) and scope of the security breach, and implementing additional controls and monitoring to prevent it from happening again.

Lastly, you must keep your BlackBerry device security infrastructure up to date, as mentioned in the chapter overview. You can provide yourself additional peace of mind by regularly monitoring and controlling access to the BlackBerry device environment, as well as investigating anomalies and correcting security issues when they arise. We highly recommend monthly vulnerability scans of the environment to ensure the patching and configuration adjustments remain effective and successful. Evaluate, patch/harden, scan/verify, and repeat.

However, just because you are performing your due diligence does not guarantee you will be breach-free; what it does give you is defensibility. Since many high-security companies are using BlackBerry devices, it would also stand to reason that those companies are a bigger target, and therefore will be the victims of more targeted attacks and more often. When there is a breach, your well-known and documented attempts at due diligence will demonstrate a culture of compliance and competence. It will be easier to make the argument that you were simply the victim of bad luck.

With the enterprise infrastructure in place, the security of your BlackBerry device population is controlled with your BlackBerry Administration Service. Keep in mind that by default, there is no security applied, so you will need to implement security policies on the devices that align with and enforce your company's information security policies. For more information about available policies, please reference the BlackBerry website. While browsing the website, check out BlackBerry Connection newsletter. Although older, an issue that was particularly helpful was found at http://www.blackberry.com/newsletters/connection/it/i410/bes_guide.shtml.

13.3 Exchange to Support iOS, Android™, and Windows® Phone

If you happen to be a Microsoft shop all the way to your e-mail infrastructure, you know that Microsoft Exchange ActiveSync 2010 has some built-in tools to help you corral your iOS, Android, and Windows Phone endpoints into basic compliance. To ensure that your architecture supports your needs, first ensure that you secure it appropriately. The example setup in Figure 13.2 illustrates using a reverse proxy in your DMZ.

As mentioned in the Blackberry Enterprise Server section, you must keep your Microsoft Exchange/ActiveSync security infrastructure up to date. Regularly monitor and control access to the environment, investigate anomalies, and be diligent about correcting security issues when they arise. As with the Blackberry Enterprise Server setup, we recommend monthly vulnerability scans of the environment to ensure the patching and configuration adjustments remain effective and successful. Evaluate, patch/harden, scan/

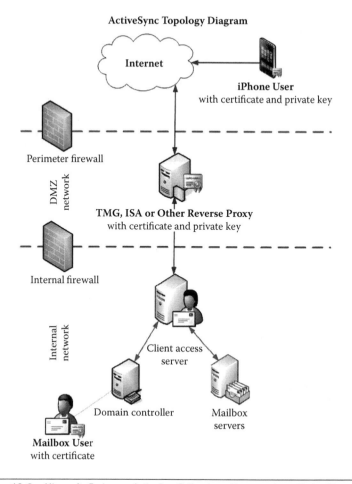

Figure 13.2 Microsoft Exchange ActiveSync® Topology Diagram, from Expta Blog. (From Jeff Guillet, "How to Securely Deploy iPhones with Exchange ActiveSync—Phase 6—End-User Deployment of the ActiveSync Profile," accessed April 28, 2012, http://www.expta.com/2010/03/how-to-securely-deploy-iphones-with_03.html.)

verify, and repeat. Your aim is still defensibility. No matter what organization you work for, your e-mail is always a delicious target to anyone with malicious intent, whether it is a disgruntled former employee (insider), your competitors, or anyone simply looking for a large cache of rich, varied data.

Microsoft TechNet and Microsoft Developer Network (MSDN) have basic material on your Exchange ActiveSync 2010 setup. We would encourage you to investigate additional resources regularly, such as Expta and other blogs and newsletters, for additional security topics. Look for Microsoft Certified Masters who also have certifications in security. After you have your architecture properly secured, you can push policies to your endpoints through ActiveSync, which has a variety of built-in controls that can be enabled, like the ones in Table 13.1 from the MSDN library.[3]

Table 13.2 shows the related MSDN table.

For additional granular control over your endpoints with Microsoft Exchange ActiveSync, you can use a mobile device management solution, referred to in Chapter 14.

References

1. Verizon Risk Group. 2012 data breach investigations report. Accessed June 9, 2012, http://www.verizonbusiness.com/resources/reports/rp_data-breach-investigations-report-2012_en_xg.pdf.
2. Research in Motion Limited. BlackBerry Enterprise Server: Placing the BlackBerry router in the DMZ version: 5.0 service pack: 3. Accessed April 7, 2012, http://docs.blackberry.com/en/admin/deliverables/25734/BlackBerry_Enterprise_Server-Security_Note--1395142-0307061517-001-5.0.3-US.pdf.
3. Matt Stehle. Provisioning, policies, remote wipe, and the allow/block/quarantine list in Exchange ActiveSync. Accessed April 7, 2012, http://msdn.microsoft.com/en-us/library/hh509085(v=exchg.140).aspx.

Table 13.1   Provisioning, Policies, Remote Wipe, and the Allow/Block/Quarantine List in Exchange ActiveSync from MSDN®

POLICY SETTING NAME	CONDITION
AllowBluetooth	Ignored if the device does not support Bluetooth.
AllowCamera	Ignored if the device does not have a camera and a camera cannot be attached to the device.
AllowDesktopSync	Ignored if the device does not support connecting to a personal computer.
AllowInternetSharing	Ignored if the device does not support sharing its Internet connection with other devices.
AllowIrDA	Ignored if the device cannot transmit or receive infrared signals.
AllowRemoteDesktop	Ignored if the device does not support connecting remotely to a personal computer.
AllowStorageCard	Ignored if the device does not support storing data on removable storage.
AllowTextMessaging	Ignored if the device is not capable of using SMS messaging.
AllowWifi	Ignored if the device does not have Wi-Fi capability.
PasswordRecoveryEnabled	Ignored if the DevicePasswordEnabled element is set to 0 (FALSE) or if the client does not support recovery passwords.
RequireStorageCardEncryption	Ignored if the device does not support removable storage. If the device supports removable storage, it must reply to this policy request based on whether it can encrypt the storage card. *At the time of this writing, not natively supported with most Android and all Windows Phone 7 devices!*
AllowSimpleDevicePassword	Ignored if the value of the DevicePasswordEnabled element is 0 (FALSE).
AlphanumericDevicePassword Required	Ignored if the value of the DevicePasswordEnabled element is 0 (FALSE).
DevicePasswordExpiration	Ignored if the value of the DevicePasswordEnabled element is 0 (FALSE).
DevicePasswordHistory	Ignored if the value of the DevicePasswordEnabled element is 0 (FALSE).
MinDevicePasswordComplex Characters	Ignored if the value of the DevicePasswordEnabled element is 0 (FALSE). Also can safely be ignored if the AlphanumericDevicePasswordRequired element is set to 0 (FALSE).
MaxDevicePasswordFailed Attempts	Ignored if the value of the DevicePasswordEnabled element is 0 (FALSE).
MinDevicePasswordLength	Ignored if the value of the DevicePasswordEnabled element is 0 (FALSE).
PasswordRecoveryEnabled	Ignored if the value of the DevicePasswordEnabled element is 0 (FALSE).

Source: From Microsoft. With permission.

Table 13.2 Expected Behavior for Additional Policy Settings

POLICY SETTING NAME	EXPECTED BEHAVIOR
AllowSimpleDevicePassword	The server does not define a simple password. In general, simple passwords can include sequential digits (1234), repeating digits (1111), letters in keyboard order (qwerty), and so on.
AlphanumericDevicePasswordRequired	If the device can only enforce a numeric PIN, the client must fail to apply this policy if it is enabled.
DeviceEncryptionEnabled	The client should encrypt any data received from the server, including e-mail messages, contacts, attachments, and so on. The client is not required to encrypt other data, such as photos or music. *At the time of this writing, not natively supported with most Android and all Windows Phone 7 devices!*
DevicePasswordEnabled	If this policy is enabled, the client must require that the user enter a password before accessing any data obtained from the server, including e-mail messages, contacts, attachments, and so on.
MaxDevicePasswordFailedAttempts	Specifies the number of consecutive attempts a user can make to enter the correct password for the device. After this number of attempts, the device must wipe all data obtained from the server. The device can (and should) implement a mechanism to prevent accidental button presses from causing a device wipe.
MaxEmailBodyTruncationSize	Specifies the maximum size (in kilobytes) at which to truncate e-mail messages when synchronized to the client. The client must not allow the user to choose a value larger than this setting. This value does not restrict the size of items returned by the ItemOperations command. The device can download the full items.
MaxEmailHTMLBodyTruncationSize	Specifies the maximum size (in kilobytes) at which to truncate HTML e-mail messages when synchronized to the client. The device must not allow the user to choose a value larger than this setting. This value does not restrict the size of items returned by the ItemOperations command. The device can download the full items.
MaxInactivityTimeDeviceLock	Specifies the length of time (in seconds) that the device can be inactive before the password is required to reactivate it. The user can choose a value that is smaller than this, but cannot choose a value that is larger.

(continued)

Table 13.2   Expected Behavior for Additional Policy Settings (continued)

POLICY SETTING NAME	EXPECTED BEHAVIOR
PasswordRecoveryEnabled	A recovery password is a second password that can be used to unlock the device if the user forgets the original password. When the user enters the recovery password, the client should prompt the user to create a new password immediately. The client should then create a new recovery password and send it to the server by using the "Settings" command as soon as possible. This is not technically a policy, because the client can still synchronize even if the device does not send a recovery password to the server. The purpose of this setting is to indicate to the client whether the server is willing to store a recovery password for the client. If the value for this policy is zero, the client should not send a recovery password to the server.

14

THE MOBILE CLIENT ITSELF

14.1 Overview

While we security practitioners have been working feverishly over the last 10 years to secure our traditional endpoints, our users have become less invested in their no-fun company laptop, and more enthralled with their smart phone or tablet. With the company laptop, you won the difficult battle of deploying appropriate controls: whole-disk encryption, data leakage prevention, group policy–controlled everything. When you weren't looking, users started working on their other devices more and more; then, one fateful day, your gadget-happy executive attended a big meeting with an iPad to take notes and a new battle began. It was just a matter of time before people started talking about data breaches with unprotected smart phones and tablets.

Here's just a taste of what we're in for with smart phones and tablets: by 2014, for just *browsing*, mobile Internet usage is projected to overtake desktop Internet usage; currently, mobile Internet usage is for socializing,[1] but that is likely to change as users slowly shed their laptops. An interesting infographic from 2011, showing our current vs. future state, can be found on Digital Buzz Blog.

Apple has sold nearly 180 million iPhones worldwide since the iPhone's initial launch.[2] Google's Android OS is growing at an astonishing rate year on year, and carriers now activate over 900,000 Android devices a day, in more than 40 countries.[3]

14.2 Tablet and Smart Phone Security Issues

Security practitioners over the past 5 to 10 years have witnessed the coming of the *tablet and smart phone revolution*, which led to the following migraines:

- Bring your own device (BYOD)
- Lack of encryption

- Lack of good authentication and password controls
- Unfiltered mobile applications
- Saying no is a tricky business
- Updating mobile standards and searching for solutions
- Performing sanity testing
- Garnering executive support and the big win

14.3 Bring Your Own Device (BYOD)

The first problem that comes to mind due to the explosive growth of smart phones and tablets is not only the mix of company and personal devices, but the mix of company and personal data on both types of devices. What's the main culprit? That would be the bring your own device (BYOD) permissiveness of today's work culture.

To add to your unease, users were purchasing their own smart phones and tablets and bringing them to work, mixing personal data with business data on that device before you even had a chance to let your department's stance be known. They were once again able to browse the Internet freely and post whatever they wanted online, using social media and online data storage. They were playing games on company time. They discovered how to connect to your mail server and started receiving company e-mails with sensitive attachments. What happens when this user loses that unprotected smart phone or leaves the company? Do you have a right to data on that phone? Had you thought of this situation in advance to create appropriate administrative and technical controls?

Some major companies have provided stipends so that employees can bring their own devices and use them for work, citing potential savings in cap-ex and op-ex, but this is not an ideal situation for security. Also, as you may have already suspected, your legal department feels uneasy about seizing employees' personal devices or retrieving company data off personally owned equipment, should it become necessary. Many attorneys consider this a legal gray area. Excellent, now you have another problem: e-discovery. Let's explore this problem statement a little more.

One of your C-level executives has been using her personally owned smart phone for a couple years now, and her device handles both personal and company data. She is unexpectedly named in a lawsuit and the attorneys decide that collection from smart phones is in scope for this case. How are you going to retrieve just relevant case data off the smart phone without violating her privacy or without having an adverse effect on her own data? Are you going to seize her smart phone while legal studies the situation and your IT support staff figures out how to browse around and collect the necessary files? What if she decides to take another job out of state? Based on my personal experience and common sense, she's going to have a huge problem with this situation. One possible solution is to employ a mobile device management (MDM) tool that gives you a degree of monitoring and control over the data on your smart phones and tablets. Two such examples of an MDM are Mobile Iron and AirWatch. No matter what vendors you interview, keep in mind that not all mobile OSs are created equally. *The degree of control that an MDM has over the device depends on the mobile OS and the device in question.* Fully explore whether each control can be implemented for each device type you've allowed in your organization.

Speaking of adversely affecting personal data, let's imagine that the same C-level executive instead leaves her smart phone in a cab, or her tablet in first class, but she does the right thing according to your acceptable use policy: she reports it to your helpdesk. You've thoughtfully instructed your helpdesk to perform a remote wipe on lost or stolen phones. Congratulations—you've just erased the photos of her daughter's birthday party, along with her audio notes for her new book. We cannot stress enough how much trouble this situation could bring for you.

Generally speaking, if you are forced to support personal devices, you must do two things:

1. You must have your users agree to your security controls and rules, or not use their personal devices for work.
2. You must find a way to segregate personal data from the company data. The industry term for this is *containerization.*

When searching for your perfect mobile device management system, or when just implementing the technical controls with your mail server, make this your priority. One example of this technical control could be the product TouchDown by NitroDesk, which creates an encrypted container around Microsoft Exchange data on

Android phones. Exchange data can be "wiped" while leaving the other data intact and users cannot move the data around to avoid the control. Additionally, depending on the mobile OS and the MDM, you may be able to retrieve the files or information needed from that e-discovery request. Although an MDM will be expensive and there is a learning curve for both administrators and users, it is worth it to have a tool that's keeping pace with the changing mobile landscape. Shop around and ask your vendors to help you put together a compelling presentation based on your current business cases.

Important Note: At the time of this writing, there is no device encryption support for Windows Phone 7! We recommend that you do not allow it to connect to your company resources until there is either native support or a software shim to enforce encryption. Additionally, only a subset of policies is currently supported. Windows Phone 7 offers much in the way of productivity, as it is currently very useful for accessing Microsoft Office documents; however, we still take issue with the still maturing security offerings.

14.4 Lack of Encryption

Who's requiring encryption on your smart phones and tablets? A better question would be, "Who's not?" If it's not one state (Massachusetts), it'll be one of the other 50, and if it's not one or more of the states, it'll be one of your big customers; if not customers (unlikely), it will be your very own Chief Information Security Officer (CISO), who wants to publish an updated information security policy set. The need for encryption is inescapable, and the best thing for everyone to do is to accept it and facilitate it. The good news is that many companies are working on this problem and some have an eye toward Federal Information Security Management Act (FISMA) compliance to widen the adoption of their solution. The newer versions of Apple's iOS offer hardware encryption for the devices, and as mentioned earlier, applications like TouchDown can containerize company data on Android devices, many of which do not offer native encryption. None of the solutions are technically perfect, but when you implement a thoughtful solution and make a best effort to do so correctly, it puts you in a very good, very defensible position should a breach occur with a smart phone or tablet afterward. So that you don't undo some of your progress, ensure that you forbid smart phones and tablets that don't currently have a solution for encryption. Perform regular audits and educate your users about only using approved devices to access company data. The bottom line is if you haven't implemented encryption with these devices, you want to make it a high priority this year. Forbid any device where encryption of company data is not easily accomplished. Remain open to testing newer versions of the mobile OS/device when improvements are (supposedly) made.

14.5 Lack of Good Authentication and Password Controls

It is extremely unfortunate that PIN codes are the main security control on mobile devices and tablets, if they are implemented at all. Furthermore, your users will balk at the idea of you implementing the same kind of robust password policy you have for computers on their smart phone or tablet. You will simply not be able to accomplish this. Your security is essentially reduced to a four-digit guess. Do you know what the most common four-digit PIN codes are? Unfortunately, many people do, but who needs to guess? An episode of accidental shoulder surfing will expose the easy PIN code, which will probably not rotate for a while, if at all. The recommendation here is to implement stricter controls with quicker PIN/password rotation, lockout, etc., as well as the ability to remotely wipe the device. Going a step further to address this challenge would involve a product like MyIdentity by Trustwave, which offers two-factor authentication options to mitigate the risk. Above all, conduct regularly occurring user education and stress the importance of securing smart phones and tablets. Engage your users as partners in the fight against unwanted data leakage, which can have disastrous consequences for everyone at the company.

In addition to PIN problems, it is guaranteed that a small number of your users will run into issues when their e-mail/network password changes. If they do not change that password quickly enough in the "Settings" area of the phone, there is a chance that the device will continue to try the old password with the mail server, possibly locking out the account. Although informed IT users know this situation has nothing to do with your PIN requirement, you will likely be implicated in a shadowy conspiracy to waste important people's time. You will have users calling you, e-mailing you, and stopping by your desk regularly. The only thing you can do in this situation is ensure that your helpdesk is trained to patiently walk the user through the scenario of resetting the e-mail password successfully. Instruct your user: immediately before he or she rotates his or her network password, have him or her put the smart phone or tablet in "airplane mode." After the network password has been changed, instruct the user to go to the mobile device's "Settings" area and change the network password there before taking the device out of "airplane mode." Training your end users on proper device management should be a part of your overall IT program.

14.6 Unfiltered Mobile Apps

With regard to security, 2011 was a tough year for Google. At first, things started off well for it; Android devices were growing in popularity and adoption, and they were enjoying the emerging backlash against all things Apple, but due to Google's hands-off attitude with the Google Play, dozens of malicious applications were downloaded by thousands of users. This caused a lot of negative press for Google at a critical growth period. Some organizations that would have adopted Android smart phones and tablets as their standard backed away from them altogether and moved toward Apple. Today, Google can now flip a kill switch and render the malicious apps unusable, once spotted, but the fact that it occurred in the first place, followed by days of radio silence and scrambling, should make all security practitioners a little wary. A positive aspect of Google's openness with regard to Google Play is that there have been antivirus/antimalware apps ready for download for quite a while now; some examples are Antivirus Free by AVG and Lookout by Lookout Mobile Security. However, when shopping around at Google Play, ensure that you are downloading the correct application from the verified vendor, instead of a malware version of it!

Apple's App Store appears to be in a slightly better position. With the control of a benevolent totalitarian regime, Apple exercises more control over apps downloaded from its store; it is suggested that Apple performs application scans or evaluations on these applications before the public can download them. Not only that, but it is widely believed that (non-jail-broken) iOS devices are protected from malicious application behavior with effective sandboxing. While this security practitioner has a difficult time accepting a well-recited line like that one from any vendor, there are some antimalware apps that are quietly starting to emerge for iOS, such as Intego. At some point, Apple will allow antimalware protection to flourish, and that will be an added layer of security on a relatively secure platform.

Instead of completely trusting any one company to handle security, consider adding on some cloud-based mobile device protection as insurance if you can't afford a full-blown MDM solution that can maintain a list of whitelisted applications.

14.7 Saying No Is a Tricky Business

Have you ever tried telling your CEO that he (1) cannot use his own device for work, (2) must use a company smart phone or tablet that complies with all controls, or (3) cannot have an exception? How did that conversation go? The problem with this situation is an age-old one: the security practitioner is once again viewed as the fun killer, the opposite of an innovator. You're a PC. As your executive reminds you that in five years, everyone will have a smart phone or tablet that controls every aspect of his or her life from birth to death, your mind races because you've heard this hype talk from him and many others (mostly vendors, who have been talking to him). You remember when laptops were starting to take off and what you did to secure that problem. Good for you.

14.8 Updating Mobile Standards and Searching for Solutions

The very first order of business to address this challenge is a comprehensive set of well-socialized and published mobile standards. The type of data your company handles, as well as your existing policy and standard set, will determine what your new mobile standards look like. Ensure that your holistic solution covers the following general areas:

- Administrative controls:
  - Acceptable use policy, which employees read and sign, to include company's instructions and stance regarding:

- Personal devices and company data
- Reporting lost or stolen devices
- Right to monitor, control, and delete any data (or company data) on the device
- Right to apply updates (security and otherwise) as needed
- Consequences for not adhering to policy, which should include a phrase like "up to and including termination"
  - Ongoing, mandatory education for employees that reminds them of:
    - Acceptable user policy details
    - Protection for company devices, including upholding and understanding all security features
    - Consequences for not adhering to policy
- Technical controls, ability to control:
  - What devices are allowed to access company data and how that access is granted
  - Encryption of both the transport layer (in motion) and the device, or at least of company data (at rest)
  - A robust password policy that covers length, complexity, rotation, timeout/reentry, history, minimum, lockout, and wipe
  - Disabling certain features, like Bluetooth, Infrared, and Wi-Fi
  - Whether to implement security services like antivirus, etc.
  - Lost or stolen phones, remote wipe
  - Security and version updates
- Support staff; ensure that they are well-trained in the areas of:
- Educating users on a regular basis about why the company is doing this and its importance, possibility citing regulatory or customer requirements
- Assisting users with various challenges, which you outline for them
- Administering the technical controls and keeping policies straight

Finally, when you're ready to explore some solutions to see whether they meet your requirements per mobile OS, group your long list of requirements in a meaningful way so that you can see how each vendor stacks up against all others. Table 14.1 is a sample requirements matrix, but you will no doubt create your own set of requirements on which you can compare each vendor.

14.9 Performing Sanity Testing

Once you know which MDM or control set you are going to use, ensure that you test and record whether the controls are enforced and how they are enforced on the devices. Since you are getting close to setting a new policy at this point, persuade at least one influential executive and one influential, vocal objector into the test policy group. Be responsive to your testers and realize these stakeholders are one of the keys to your success. Have each of them carefully observe and record his or her recollection of how the control was executed on his or her device. Listen to their observations and feedback carefully.

At the end of your testing cycles, you can roll up the individual test scripts into a summary document for your records. Here is an example rollup:

> **Test overview:** This stage of testing should include your mobile security requirements, like the example below:
>
> Testers, please:
>
> 1. Confirm six-character alphanumeric password with no complex character and no simple sequences allowed.
> 2. Confirm device encryption + storage card encryption if applicable to phone.
> 3. Confirm password rotation period = 30 days.
> 4. Confirm password history = 10.
> 5. Confirm screen lock + password reentry after 5 minutes.
> 6. Confirm local wipe at four failed password entry attempts.
> 7. Confirm remote wipe before test period ends (initiated by administrator at appointed date/time).

Table 14.1   Mobile Device Management Requirements

MOBILE OS NAME GOES HERE	OS NAME	OS NAME	OS NAME

E-MAIL CONTROLS
Edit refresh interval for any policy changes?
Can set limits on attachments?
Specify message format, for example, HTML?
E-mail/calendar/task/contact syncing?

AUTHENTICATION OPTIONS
Can require two-factor authentication?
Require password/PIN?
Minimum password length $= x$?
Alphanumeric passwords?
Require a minimum number of complex
  characters?
Allow simple password if needed?
Inactivity lockout after x minutes?
Set maximum failed password attempts $= x$?
Password expiration $= x$ days?
Password minimum age $> x$ (hour, day)?
Enforce password history $= x$?
Enable password recovery/administrative reset?

ENCRYPTION OPTIONS
Disable support for older encryption?
Enable device encryption?
Enable storage card encryption?
Require SSL encryption for web/application?
TLS and WTLS support?

GENERAL DEVICE CONTROLS
Allow and disallow nonprovisionable device?
Can remotely wipe device?
Can locally wipe device?
Can selectively wipe device?
Disable removable storage?
Disable desktop ActiveSync (Exchange)?
Disable camera?
Disable Bluetooth?
Disable SMS/MMS text messaging?
GPS tracking of phone user?

NETWORK AND SECURITY CONTROLS
Have the ability to use antivirus protection?

(continued)

Table 14.1   Mobile Device Management Requirements (continued)

MOBILE OS NAME GOES HERE	OS NAME	OS NAME	OS NAME
Have the ability to use integrated firewall?			
Allow Internet sharing from device?			
Allow desktop sharing from device?			
APPLICATION AND SECURITY CONTROLS			
Allow noncompany e-mail?			
Disable POP3/IMAP4 e-mail?			
Allow browsing?			
Allow unsigned applications?			
Application whitelist?			
Application blacklist?			
Allow Windows file share access?			
Allow Windows SharePoint access?			

Timeline: Testing is set to begin on (January 5) and end on (February 15).

Results: All testers submitted individual test scripts after testing concluded; the summary of their results is listed in line with the testers' mobile OS/phone combinations in Table 14.2.

14.10 Garnering Executive Support and the Big Win

If you were very clever, you persuaded your executive and vocal objector to participate in the security testing, and they have faithfully completed their test scripts, and are now helping you to champion this cause with their coworkers. You will know what drawbacks and challenges to expect because your testing cycles also served as opportunities to air complaints. Your executive and vocal objector are both moving toward the acceptance phase, and they will be helpful in assisting others to do the same.

Take advantage of this period of illumination and draft a company-wide memo of the upcoming changes: what problems these new controls solve for the company, what users can expect, what will actually change, and where to report issues. Partner with your executive champion and CISO to distribute this memo, and to meet with other executives about the upcoming changes. Executives do not like you messing with their devices and have likely petitioned for exceptions

Table 14.2 Information Security Test Script for Mobile OS

MOBILE OS TYPE	TESTER NAME	RECORDED RESULTS AND ISSUES
Mobile OS type 1, phone A	Tester A reporting	1. Confirmed appropriate password is required; phone refused simple sequence.
		2. Confirmed phone's encryption message. Storage card encryption confirmed. Need device to decrypt the new file created for this test.
		3. Confirmed that phone prompted for new password after 30th day—entered new password.
		4. Confirmed password history by changing password and attempting to reuse passwords—forced to enter new.
		5. Confirmed that phone enforces password reentry after 5 minutes.
		6. Confirmed local wipe occurs after four failed password attempts—phone resets to default and setup information, and activation was necessary again.
		7. Admin sent wipe request to the phone—confirmed that phone reset to default settings. Needed to reactivate and set up the phone again.
Mobile OS type 2, phone B	Tester B reporting	*Most* items in compliance: 1. No simple sequence allowed—was forced to enter the correctly formatted password.
		2. Device is using hardware encryption, and storage cards are *not* a change option for this phone.
		3. Prompted for password after 30th day—entered new password.
		4. Password history = 10 was enforced.
		5. Was prompted for password after 5 minutes.
		6. After four failed attempts, phone is disabled for 1 minute except for emergency calls (see numbers 8 and 9 below).
		7. Remote wipe: wiped to factory settings.
		8. If the password is entered *correctly* after the 1-minute lockout, the phone does not wipe. The failed attempt resets the phone.
		9. If the password is entered *incorrectly* following the 1-minute lockout, the phone is wiped to factory settings and disabled until synced.

in the past. This is an example of an executive who is living with your security controls, and is espousing them on your behalf.

Partner with your vocal objector to capture a full list of FAQs, and then ensure that you have trained support staff to assist with this transition period for a successful implementation.

Remember that your most powerful weapons in this battle are education, buy-in, and consistency. We recommend that you create a small committee, whose membership spans different user groups, selecting influential members where you can. This committee can be called together occasionally to discuss new mobile device challenges, as well as to help you with testing. Keep your committee members well informed and encourage them to do the same with their fellow users. With a lot of planning and a little luck, you will be able to better control the smart phones and tablets in your company.

References

1. Aden Hepburn. Infographic: Mobile statistics, stats, & facts 2011. Accessed June 16, 2012, http://www.digitalbuzzblog.com/2011-mobile-statistics-stats-facts-marketing-infographic/.
2. Horace Dediu. Apple sold more iOS devices in 2011 than all the Macs it sold in 28 years. Accessed June 16, 2012, http://www.asymco.com/2012/02/16/ios-devices-in-2011-vs-macs-sold-it-in-28-years/.
3. Wade Johnston. Mobile marketing stats and facts for 2011. Accessed June 16, 2012, http://modular4kc.com/2011/04/04/mobile-marketing-stats-and-facts-for-2011/.

15

CONNECTING TO ENTERPRISE AND THIRD-PARTY APPLICATIONS FROM MOBILE DEVICES

15.1 Overview

Mobile devices within an enterprise represent a large area of positive opportunities for organizations. Not only do mobile users feel more connected with each other, but they are also more productive, leading to more customer engagement and higher satisfaction. The mobile device is not only here to stay, but will accelerate the way corporations manage and connect to their customers and workforce, building a stronger, more connected community. Connecting mobile devices to enterprise systems might be as simple as allowing workers to connect to the corporate network, or as deep as creating custom applications to drive increased sales or other efficiencies. Each mobile device platform will have its own way of connecting to a secure enterprise environment, but they all fall into the two following categories:

- Connect to the corporate network through either a virtual private network (VPN) or a secure Wi-Fi connection (IPsec VPN is recommended)
- Use a built-in or custom application to connect to an enterprise service or website

15.2 Connecting to Exchange

Connecting a tablet or smart phone to Microsoft Exchange falls into the second category: use a built-in application to connect. The most basic way to connect a mobile device to Exchange is through ActiveSync 2010. Layering a mobile device management system affords you more visibility and granularity of control. Refer to these headings in the book for more information on this topic:

- "Architecture to Support iOS, Android, and Windows Phone" (Chapter 13)
- "The Mobile Client Itself" (Chapter 14)

Important Note: At this time we do not recommend connecting Windows Phone 7 to your company's Exchange environment. Wait for information on Windows 8, as it is designed with mobility in mind.

15.3 Connecting via VPN

Connecting via VPN to access company resources falls into the first category, where you allow your users to access company resources over a connection that you secure and control (Table 15.1). As security practitioners, one of the most challenging aspects of our jobs is that users will demand that everything is available instantly on their smart

Table 15.1 Connecting Mobile Devices to VPN

MOBILE OS	SUGGESTIONS
iOS	Apple offers built-in VPN clients, located under General ◊ Network ◊ VPN. The IPsec VPN from Cisco is preferable if you can support it; you will need to work with your network security team on the firewall and VPN concentrator settings. Additionally, Layer 2 Tunneling Protocol (L2TP) and Point-to-Point Tunneling Protocol (PPTP) configurations are also supported. PPTP is generally not recommended.
Android	VPN setup will vary by device, but should be available under Settings ◊ Wireless and Network Settings ◊ VPN Settings ◊ Add VPN. The L2TP/IPsec VPN options are preferred, with certificate-based L2TP/IPsec VPN as the best overall option (versus preshared key).
Windows Phone 7	Currently, there is no VPN client available for Windows Phone 7. At this time, we do not recommend that you allow company data to be accessed on Windows Phone 7 until both the VPN and encryption issues are properly addressed by Microsoft.
BlackBerry	Example: If using a BlackBerry Playbook, go to Settings ◊ Security ◊ Add New (VPN Profile). Using IPsec with Internet Key Exchange (IKE), one of two types of authentication to access the network can be employed: preshared keys and digital certificates "Xauth PSK," where digital certificates will be easier for you to manage with a large user base.*

* Dan Kennedy, "How to Setup Blackberry Playbook VPN," accessed June 23, 2012, http://aussecurity. wordpress.com/2011/04/19/how-to-setup-playbook-vpn/.

phones and tablets, much the way they currently experience with their company laptops. If your users haven't yet asked for a VPN connection from their smart phones and tablets, they will soon. Before giving this type of access to your users, you must have your mobile device security in place. It's also very helpful to have it standardized on a mobile device/OS that allows you to uniformly enforce your policies. For more information on this topic, refer to the following heading in the book: "The Mobile Client Itself" (Chapter 14).

Currently, iOS appears to be ahead of most of its competitors with regards to security and offering IPsec VPN, which suggests to us that Apple is vying for the top spot with enterprise users. The control that Apple maintains over its hardware and software enables it to move faster with regard to many endeavors and is encouraging to security practitioners. We recommend that you set up your users with IPsec VPN using the latest version of iOS. If your organization does not support IPsec VPN, consider an upgrade path so that you can support it.

At this writing, Android is temporarily suffering from a lack of uniformity and strong security between the myriad Android devices, their flavors of mobile operating systems, and the VPN clients. In many cases, there is no practical support among many popular gateways. There are vendors who are working quickly to remedy this situation, and we are looking forward to IPsec VPN being fully supported (hopefully) within the next year. One such vendor, who is working to remedy this situation, is NCP Communications.[1] We do not recommend that you decrement your network security just to support a particular device; however, if necessary, you can use a VPN configuration with slightly less security. Keep in mind that files transferred from your company network to the Android device's storage card will not be encrypted, unless the user chooses to encrypt the file himself or herself. Chances are he or she will not opt to do this.

Windows Phone 7 does not currently support a VPN connection at the time of this writing, but Microsoft is working on it, along with other key enterprise features, for future releases (Windows Phone 8 or later).

BlackBerry has offered excellent security options for a long time now, and if using a BlackBerry device, you can take advantage of its mature security offerings. Secure VPN is not an issue.

15.4 Connecting to Microsoft SharePoint® 2010 or Later

Microsoft SharePoint 2010 is a web-based collaboration platform designed to provide a variety of features to enterprise end users in an easy-to-use, self-service manner. Collaborating on a shared SharePoint list or document library is available via a standard web browser interface. The overall SharePoint interface runs well on most modern browsers, but as you would expect, it runs best in Microsoft's own Internet Explorer web browser. Mobile devices normally connect to the public Internet via their cellular or Wi-Fi connections; accessing the enterprise SharePoint server behind the firewall needs to be taken into consideration. This is normally done by forcing users to connect to the corporate VPN prior to accessing the SharePoint site, or by configuring a mobile proxy system such as Microsoft's Mobile Device Manager or BlackBerry Enterprise Server, or by positioning SharePoint on a segment of the corporate extranet network, which allows direct connections from the public Internet. If a device is already connected to the corporate network via a Wi-Fi connection, there are normally no additional configuration steps necessary for those devices to access SharePoint.

Although the Microsoft SharePoint 2010 platform offers a large variety of capabilities and features, many users tend to work with only a subset of features from their mobile devices, primarily viewing and retrieving documents, viewing lists, and viewing reports or other metrics. These functions work best within a tablet environment where additional screen space is available for users to see larger amounts of data than on a mobile phone device. Many smart phone users find that their tiny screens are insufficient for viewing a full-fledged SharePoint website, and Microsoft provides mobile-ready screens to help users on these devices more easily navigate the system. Even with this lightweight interface, many find it difficult to navigate the often terse and limited navigation system on their tiny screens and choose to install an application specifically designed to ease the interaction between the SharePoint 2010 system and the mobile device user. There are a variety of applications available for each of the various device platforms. For example, SharePlus: SharePoint Mobile Client is a popular application for both Android and iOS devices, SilverDust for BlackBerry handsets, and SharePoint Workspace Mobile is included within the

Office Mobile Hub of Windows Phones. Each offers a simplified user experience allowing easy connections to SharePoint and navigation to view sites, lists, documents, etc.

Your enterprise data are your company's competitive advantage and SharePoint 2010 allows users to store and access all of them from their mobile devices. This might seem like a security practitioner's worst nightmare, but if you've already established a secure mobile device policy as outlined earlier, securing mobile access to SharePoint is already (mostly) done. Since all users will access SharePoint via a web browser interface or a custom application that uses the SharePoint web services, ensure that communication is secured via a Secure Socket Layer (SSL) certificate matching your organization's SSL encryption policies. This level of security provides end-to-end encryption of the data, but does not implicitly provide encryption of the data on the remote device; you should be aware that the mobile device might cache sensitive information local to the device. The recommendation here is to review your mobile device security policies to ensure proper device locking and remote wipe capabilities in the event the mobile device is lost or stolen.

Microsoft SharePoint 2010 access is controlled via a fully implemented role-based security paradigm, allowing for very granular control over all aspects of the SharePoint environment. Once your organization has established its SharePoint access control plan, all sites, subsites, lists, document libraries, etc., are governed by these controls, and are passed to both the web user experience and the mobile application experience. For example, if you have access to sensitive data on a SharePoint site via your desktop browser, you will also have the same access via your mobile device.

Table 15.2 lists the default permission levels for team sites in SharePoint Server 2010. Ensure that you have implemented the appropriate permission levels for your users and the data they are accessing.

15.5 Connecting to a Desktop or Server

Another request from your users will be the ability to remotely connect to their desktop(s) or their server(s): a remote desktop request. This is probably not something they will be doing very often; the combination of working with the smaller screen, VPN, lack of a mouse,

Table 15.2   Permissions Table from TechNet

PERMISSION LEVEL	DESCRIPTION	PERMISSIONS INCLUDED BY DEFAULT
Limited access	Allows access to shared resources in the website so that the users can access an item within the site. Designed to be combined with fine-grained permissions to give users access to a specific list, document library, folder, list item, or document, without giving them access to the entire site. Cannot be customized or deleted.	• View application pages • Browse user information • Use remote interfaces • Use client integration features • Open

Read	View pages, list items, and download documents.	• Limited access permissions, plus:
		  • View items
		  • Open items
		  • View versions
		  • Create alerts
		  • Use self-service site creation
		  • View pages

Contribute	View, add, update, and delete items in the existing lists and document libraries.	• Read permissions, plus:
		  • Add items
		  • Edit items
		  • Delete items
		  • Delete versions
		  • Browse directories
		  • Edit personal user information
		  • Manage personal views
		  • Add/remove personal web parts
		  • Update personal web parts

Design	View, add, update, delete, approve, and customize items or pages in the website.	• Approve permissions, plus:
		  • Manage lists
		  • Add and customize pages
		  • Apply themes and borders
		  • Apply style sheets

Full control	Allows full control of the scope.	All permissions

Source: MSDN, "User Permissions and Permission Levels (SharePoint Server 2010)," accessed June 9, 2012, http://technet.microsoft.com/en-us/library/cc721640.aspx. Used with permission from Microsoft.

and overall slowness will tax their patience and make them reach for their company-issued laptop.

For iOS users, RDP/VNC products such as PocketCloud by Wyse Technology, Inc., will allow users to connect to a target computer where RDP is enabled/allowed. For added security, the upgraded version offers RDP 256-bit NLA/TLS encryption, whereas the free version does not.

For Android users, Splash Top is the *de facto* standard, but users can use PocketCloud as well. With Splash Top, security is dependent upon the connection type (inherited). It is recommended that you have users connect to the network via your preferred VPN connection first, and then use Splash Top to connect to the target computer. Other applications available include RemoteDesktopClientbyXtralogic, Inc., which offers various security features for secure access, such as SSL/TLS and network level authentication.

For your Windows Phone 7 users, we do not recommend that you allow them to connect to company assets or any sensitive data from their smart phone or tablet until Microsoft addresses at least the VPN and device encryption issues. In the event you still allow users to connect using their Windows Phone 7, there are many apps available from the Windows Marketplace that provide standard RDP connections.

For your BlackBerry Playbook users, apps like Remote Desktop for BlackBerry Playbook are available to allow the device to connect to assets like a Windows 7 machine. As with the other devices, we recommend that users first connect to the network via your preferred VPN connection before using Remote Desktop for BlackBerry Playbook.

Additionally, there is a different class of products that can help users connect to these assets. These products require agents to be installed on the target computer, which circumvents the VPN connection, but purportedly guarantees a secure communication. Two such examples are GotToMyPC and LogMeIn. We do not recommend circumventing VPN unless VPN is unavailable, and the subset of users who require this access need to gain access to their desktop(s) or server(s).

15.6 Connecting to File Shares

A less popular request from your users will be for the ability to connect to company file shares. Once your remote smart phone or tablet users have securely connected through VPN, they should be able to browse the network much the way they do with their VPN-connected laptop.

- iOS users can download and use FileBrowser by Stratospherix, Ltd., which allows access to network folders.
- Android users can use ES File Explorer, available on Google Play.
- Windows Phone 7.5 users can use ShareFolder by Kimodosoft, available on Marketplace.
- Blackberry Enterprise Server 5 users can browse network files provided the administrator sets it up on the BlackBerry Web Administration console. Browse to Servers and Components ◊ BlackBerry Domain ◊ Component View ◊ MDS Connection Service. Click the "File" tab and select the option "Edit Component."[2]

However, due to small screen size and overall slowness of the remote connection, most users will not have the patience to navigate to the network this way to locate the needed file share.

For your on-premises smart phone or tablet users, they can connect to your user network to access file shares; add the user/device to your existing wireless group. Ensure that you are logging and monitoring this user traffic with an intrusion prevention and detection system (IPS/IDS) device, especially if you allow bring your own device (BYOD) or allow your users to download and install any application on their smart phone or tablet without restrictions.

15.7 Connecting to or Installing Third-Party Applications

Connecting a tablet or smart phone to enterprise applications is generally far safer than connecting it to third-party applications that you don't secure or control. Mobile devices need to be protected from malicious code and attempts to steal data. While Apple's App Store makes a concerted attempt to limit or eliminate malicious applications, it cannot stop all of them. Google Play has just begun to control the quality of applications in the store. Refer to the following heading in this book for more information on this topic: "The Mobile Client Itself" (Chapter 14).

References

1. H Developer. Universal IPSec VPN client for Android 4.0. Accessed June 23, 2012, http://www.h-online.com/security/news/item/Universal-IPSec-VPN-client-for-Android-4-0-1543230.html.
2. BrightPoint. Accessing remote file shares with BES 5. Accessed June 9, 2012, http://blog.brightpointuk.co.uk/accessing-remote-file -shares-bes-5.

16

CREATING SECURE
MOBILE APPLICATIONS

16.1 Mobile Application Development in Your Organization

Prepare to meet a little resistance when you start the discussions regarding mobile application security. Some detractors might say that this mobile application is "just a simple front end" to a current web application. In reality, your mobile application development should closely follow your established software development life cycle (SDLC) process, mandated by company policy, audited by your internal information security department, and tested by external information security teams or auditors. The SDLC must contain at least one security checkpoint at every relevant phase. But, for an added level of confidence while designing, developing, and deploying the new application, the information security department should partner with the development team, rendering security requirements that are incorporated into each stage of the process. In fact, it is best practice for this partnership to exist from the beginning, providing input and remediation feedback before moving to the next stage. Even though the developers own the application development, the information security department must actively consult with the development team, to guide them. Every group, every stakeholder has something to gain by involving information security from the very beginning. If you are interested in more detailed information regarding the SDLC and how you should integrate security into every phase, you can reference (ISC)² publications, or the relevant National Institute of Standards and Technology (NIST) publications.

16.2 Start with the Stakeholders

An (ISC) reference, "The Ten Best Practices for Secure Software Development," by Mano Paul, discusses the importance of engaging the right stakeholders before moving forward with the project (Figure 16.1). The group of stakeholders is much larger than you might think, encompassing the following individuals or groups:

- Top management: Getting executive management support may be fundamental to establishing a top-down mandate for secure application development for the company. Work with the chief general counsel, chief compliance officer, or chief security officer to establish the importance of secure coding practices for the company.
- Business unit (BU) heads: Make sure you get the executive support from the BU heads. Developers will naturally push back on security due to more pressing business needs. The BU head *can* be convinced to balance the need for compliance and security because he or she has a much more strategic view. If you've succeeded in establishing a strong mandate at the board or executive management level, obtaining BU head support should be the next logical step.

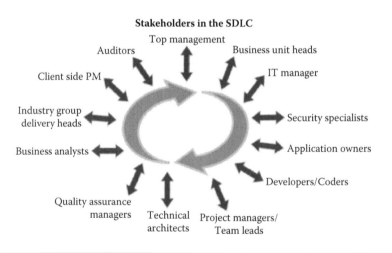

Stakeholders in the SDLC

Top management

Auditors

Business unit heads

Client side PM

IT manager

Industry group delivery heads

Security specialists

Business analysts

Application owners

Developers/Coders

Quality assurance managers

Technical architects

Project managers/ Team leads

Figure 16.1 From "The Ten Best Practices for Secure Software Development." (From Mano Paul, "The Ten Best Practice for Secure Software Development," accessed June 2, 2012, https://www.isc2.org/uploaded-Files/(ISC)2_Public_Content/Certification_Programs/CSSLP/ISC2_WPIV.pdf. With permission.)

- IT managers: These are managers of the development groups. The managers are driven by very tight timelines and have the ability to help developers prioritize. If you want the mobile apps to be developed securely, you need to change the culture at the management level. They will have the operational know-how to push the mandate down to the developers.
- Security specialists: In order for you to effectively convince coders that you know what you're talking about, you need to equip your team with specialists that can provide reasonable secure alternatives to their current way of doing things. Most developers are not adverse to doing the right thing when provided with a viable solution.
- Application owners: BU heads could be application owners, but this role could be delegated to senior development managers as well. Support from the application owner has similar weight to getting that of the BU head. The application owner has the deepest knowledge of the intricacies of the application. In complex security matters, you will need to effectively collaborate with the application owner to push your agenda through.
- Developers/coders: This is where the rubber meets the road. Getting the developers to actually code securely is the final frontier. To change culture, you need to provide the developers with a mandate from their management. You need to equip them with easy-to-use tools to examine the security of their code, preferably during the coding process. You need to solidify the right behavior by providing reasonable alternatives. You need to provide them with positive reinforcements when they do the job right. Do this over time and secure coding culture will emerge within your organization.
- Project managers/team leads: These are coordinators that have authority to prioritize. Make sure that you educate them on the importance of prioritizing information security into mobile app development.
- Technical architects: Information security components usually extend beyond the code. Technical architects are needed to look at the security of the entire solution from the endpoint to the transport, transaction, and storage mechanisms.

Work with the technical architect(s) to push the end-to-end security mandate.

- Quality assurance (QA) managers: Having the support of QA will prevent code from being published if it does not meet a certain standard. Embed your information security checklist into the QA procedures.
- Business analysts: Analysts are needed to capture requirements. Make sure that security requirements are documented. This ensures that they are incorporated into the end product.
- Industry group delivery heads: Industry decision makers have a vested interest in ensuring that software developed in their vertical is dependable and secure.
- Client-side project manager (PM): If the software is being developed for end users or another entity, the client should be engaged to specify security requirements for the end product.
- Auditors: There are a number of regulations and industry practice that advocate secure coding practices. Auditors will be measuring the development team on these standards.

Different organizations have stakeholders that carry different weights. Be sure to include the right players to establish secure coding practices for your mobile applications.

16.3 Step through the Entire SDLC

Another (ISC)² reference, "Software Assurance: A Kaleidoscope of Perspectives," by Mano Paul, discusses the elements of software security through the entire life cycle, from initiation to sunset, or, in other words, from envisioning and planning to disposal,[1] no matter what development methodology is used. Note that it does not exactly mirror the NIST publication, and that considering more than one source for guidance on security checkpoints in your SDLC can help you customize the right fit for your organization (see Table 16.1).

The relevant NIST Special Publication is 800-64 Revision 2, "Security Considerations in the System Development Life Cycle," which among other things defines the security checkpoints for each phase. The publication goes into detail regarding the major security

Table 16.1   Software Assurance: A Kaleidoscope of Perspectives

PHASE	PHASE #	STEP
Envisioning	1	Identify threat/risk vector(s)
Planning	2	Profile software
	3	Threat/risk modeling
	4	Generate security and risk requirements
Developing	5	Control check
Release	6	Handle threat/risk
Stabilization	7	Learn and educate

Source: Mano Paul, "Software Assurance: A Kaleidoscope of Perspectives," accessed June 2, 2012, https://www.isc2.org/uploadedFiles/ (ISC)-2_Public_Content/Certification_Programs/CSSLP/CSSLP_ Whitepaper_2-ONLINE(1).pdf. With permission.

activities at each stage: describing what's happening at each stage, what the expected output should be, how to synchronize, if there are any interdependencies, etc.; if it has been awhile since you last reviewed the publication, the interpretive extract in Table 16.2 should serve as a quick reminder of the security considerations in the different phases.[2]

No matter what the secure SDLC process looks like in your organization, you will also want to institute application vulnerability scans on the mobile applications before they are released into production, and then periodically after they are in production. In an ideal world, there would be a process to scan any new code that's created. Our recommendation is to create a situation that is convenient for your development staff, like an automatic scan upon code check-in, with automatically generated vulnerability reports, along with the ability to quickly and easily scan new snippets of code in an ad hoc fashion. Every two weeks to every month is a good interval.

As important as the vulnerability scans are, you should also be assigning business logic reviews of the code to your developers whenever new functionality is designed and coded. Having regularly occurring scans, with remediation on file, is essential and goes a long way in proving your organization is serious about due diligence, but nothing beats the scans in concert with contextual, human code review. Your developers will ferret out mistakes that the scan is guaranteed to miss. This in turn lowers your overall risk.

Another review you may consider on the mobile application is a third-party penetration test. The scope of the penetration test will

Table 16.2   Extract (Interpretive) from NIST Special Publication 800-64 Revision 2

DEVELOPMENT PHASE	SECURITY CONSIDERATIONS
Initiation	• Classify/categorize the data used in the mobile application and the requirements around those data, with regards to confidentiality, integrity, and availability. Consider regulatory requirements, customer requirements, as well as your own company's requirements. • Remind your development group about your company's secure coding practices.
Development/acquisition	• Ask: "What are all the ways this mobile application could be attacked?" Conduct your risk assessment, using the results to help you create additional controls. • Perform security testing. • Draft documents for certification and accreditation; draft your security architecture.
Implementation/assessment	• Monitor the mobile application as it is being placed in production; conduct security testing and certification activities. • Provide a security report.
Operations/maintenance	• Assess the mobile application's operational readiness; review the configuration. • Ensure there are processes to maintain or improve the security level of the mobile application once it's in production. Example document types needed include, but are not limited to, patching and upgrades, monitoring, incident handling, etc. • When significant changes to the mobile application are needed, reenter it into a previous phase of the SDLC. You will need to perform certain security activities again.

be based on the attack surface you identified in earlier phases of the SDLC, and the need for it will be determined on a case-by-case basis. We've noted that customers are starting to ask about the results of the last penetration test when the application handles sensitive data.

It bears restating the adage that the earlier in the process you find flaws and remediate them, the cheaper and easier it is for your organization. It will cost much more to discover and fix a flaw once your application is in production and your customers are already using it; however, it will cost you significantly more, sometimes astoundingly more, if someone other than you discovers the flaw, exploits it, and then makes a victim of your organization's customers and a sudden vacancy in your job!

Other things to consider:

- Was the mobile application classified yet? The information security department's classification of the mobile application should map to guidelines published by organizations such as Payment Card Industry (PCI) and state and federal government agencies, as well as be in line with your customer agreements and your own company's policies. Special attention should be paid during the requirements phase regarding persistence of code and some data on the smart phone or tablet meant to enhance the user experience; examine how they could be at risk. Help the business and the development team make an informed decision with regard to what can be attacked, how many records could be at risk, what the estimated price of a breach is, etc. Planning for an eventual breach is smarter than betting on a breach never happening. If you emphasize one idea with the team at every stage, let it be: How can we minimize the damage?
- Have you verified that the libraries and other third-party components your developers use are from a reputable source, providing support to your developers if needed? Are they the latest and most secure version?
- Do you have role-based access controls that segregate the different teams and their functions? Who has what access to what environment, and how often is that access reviewed and approved?
- Do you have any monitoring in place to prevent unauthorized code changes?
- How do you ensure that only certified and approved code will run in production?
- Are you outsourcing your development? If so, what is the outsourcer doing to protect your mobile application and the data? Do you have a contract in place that specifically protects your company, its data, and intellectual property? When was the last time you reviewed the outsourcer?
- Is everyone involved aware of the plan for continued security after the mobile application is in production? Continue scanning and testing the code at the proper scan interval, based on

your policies. It would be ideal if you had application security monitoring, and could detect and prevent malicious traffic to your application.

16.4 Guidelines Regarding Enterprise App Store/Google® Play

16.4.1 Overview of Infrastructure

Ideally, your homegrown App Store/Google Play architecture should look like the already secured development, QA, staging, and production environment that you use for your other applications. We won't go into the specifics of the setup; suffice it to say that if all your current environments adhere to your information security policies and follow a proper three-tiered network architecture with monitored firewalls, intrusion detection and prevention system (IDS/IPS), data leakage prevention, and encryption, and that you've implemented true segregation of data and duties, you are on the right track. Ensure that the developer workstations are locked down and located in a developer virtual local area network (VLAN).

If you have any doubts about the current infrastructure, you're probably not alone. We recommend that you perform a quick security design review of the entire setup, interviewing the different custodians and documenting that your current setup addresses all the applicable information security domains. Consider your store to be like any other public-facing offering and secure it accordingly, because it will be probed as soon as it's online. Have a short list of individually identifiable people who can publish to the store. When there is an incident, you will have your security design review on file, along with any improvements made because of information security's recommendations and any waived requirements by your senior executives, who will have to answer for their lack of support for key security controls.

16.4.2 Overview of Environment Setup and General Controls

Information security and development should partner and address the following questions:

- What types of servers are we using, and what functions do we need enabled?

- Are the different environments used secure? Who has access to what environments and how often is that reviewed/approved?
- Are we using the latest and most secure Software Development Kits (SDKs), libraries, applications, and other tools?
- Have we agreed upon a set of best practices for this effort?

16.4.3 A Note about Publishing Your Apps

Once your general concerns about the security of the environment are put aside, you will have a couple extra items to consider.

16.4.3.1 Dealing with the Apple® App Store Identify which trusted developers and development machines have access to the external agent certificate. The completed, remediated application must be compiled with this certificate. Limit access to these certificates and keep a careful eye on transfers and terminations within the development organization. We suggest that you ask your internal audit or provisioning teams for assistance in this area, so you can focus on your core competencies.

Identify the gatekeeper who sends the compiled application for publishing. This gatekeeper should sign off that all the necessary controls have been followed.

16.4.3.2 Dealing with Android's Google Play As with the section above, identify your gatekeeper who sends the completed, remediated Android application for publishing. This gatekeeper should sign off that all the necessary controls have been followed.

References

1. Mano Paul. Software assurance: A kaleidoscope of perspectives. Accessed June 2, 2012, https://www.isc2.org/uploadedFiles/(ISC)2_Public_Content /Certification_Programs/CSSLP/CSSLP_WhitePaper_2-ONLINE(1). pdf.
2. Richard Kissel, Kevin Stine, Matthew Scholl, Hart Rossman, Jim Fahlsing, and Jessica Gulick. NIST special publication 800-64 revision 2: Security considerations in the system development life cycle. Accessed June 30, 2012, http://csrc.nist.gov/publications/nistpubs/800-64-Rev2/ SP800-64-Revision2.pdf.

Index